SCANDINAVIAN INSTITUTE OF
ASIAN STUDIES MONOGRAPH SERIES

NO 6

A Symposium on
Chinese Grammar

Held at the Scandinavian Institute of Asian
Studies, Copenhagen 27-29 August 1970
under the chairmanship of Søren Egerod

Edited with transcription of the discussions
by Inga-Lill Hansson

Studentlitteratur

©Studentlitteratur, Scandinavian Institute of Asian Studies 1971
Printed in Sweden
Studentlitteratur
Lund 1971
ISBN - 91-44-06371-7

CONTENTS

PL
1021
.S9
1970

From the auditorium the following took part in the discussions:
Dr Chang Tao-wen and Fil lic Kristina Lindell from the East Asian
Institute, University of Copenhagen.

PREFACE

On August 27th-29th, 1970, the Scandinavian Institute of Asian Studies arranged a Symposium on Chinese Grammar in Copenhagen. Professor Søren Egerod was chairman of the Symposium. The participants were:

Professor Søren Egerod, East Asian Institute, University of Copenhagen
Dr A.C.Graham, School of Oriental and African Studies, London
Dr Paul Kratochvil, Faculty of Oriental Studies, University of Cambridge
Professor Göran Malmqvist, Institute of Oriental Languages, University of Stockholm
Professor Alexis Rygaloff, École Pratique des Hautes Études, Paris

It was decided during the Symposium that the papers and the discussions should be published together. The discussions after each paper were recorded on tape and the main arguments have been transcribed and edited for publishing. The colloquial style has been maintained.

The papers and discussions are arranged in the same order as they were actually held.

The transcription system chosen by each author has also been used in the discussion following the paper.

An "Index of terms" was added to Søren Egerod's paper by the editor.

Inga-Lill Hansson
editor

Paul Kratochvil

AN EXPERIMENT IN THE PERCEPTION OF PEKING DIALECT TONES

1. Introduction

According to the phonetic lore well established and continually perpetuated
in Chinese and general linguistics, the tone in Peking Dialect is exclusively, or at least predominantly a pitch feature[1]. This concept, similarly
as many others in the sphere of prosodies, is largely based on phonology:
the category is defined on phonological grounds in the first place (i.e. as
a phoneme), and then a suitable phonetic correlate is assigned to it. Not
just any correlate but one of the kind phonologists prefer: a relatively
simple, economical, and elegant component of a neat pattern. There is,
of course, no reason why the correlation should have such properties (if
indeed there is any correlation at all) but it is not fashionable among
linguists to admit this nowadays. One is perhaps somewhat disrespect-
fully reminded in this context of the youthful revolutionary who is said
(quoting Professor Mei Tsu-lin's account of the event) to have addressed
a meeting at Harvard in 1969 with the words 'these are the conclusions
upon which we base our facts'.

Nevertheless, there have been some less phonologically bound phoneticians
who suggested that pitch is not necessarily the sole and perhaps even the
predominant acoustic correlate of Peking Dialect tone[2], and that the tone
appears rather as a complex acoustic phenomenon with at least three dimensions: fundamental frequency (pitch), overall amplitude (loudness),
and time (duration). However, still next to nothing has been said about the
way this complex works internally and externally. That is, how the three
dimensions relate to each other, and precisely in what terms the complex
is perceived. For approaching questions of this kind, large-scale analysis
of speech data is obviously necessary, and this poses a number of problems
of its own. Before all, and quite apart from such elementary points as the
size and nature of the required corpus of data (acoustic phoneticians are
mostly accustomed to work with small groups of items usually predigested
into citation forms; this sort of material is patently unsuitable for the task
in question), one needs reliable criteria for recognizing what in the stream
of speech is pertinent to tones and what is not. This is not a problem of
instrumental adequacy: disregarding such relatively minor technical
questions as the precise measurement of fundamental frequency[3], the
art has now reached a state which permits accurate and quick multidimen-
sional measurements of all the relevant aspects of speech. Neither is it

necessarily a problem involving phonological considerations. Admittedly, understanding what the given text means (i.e. having an idea of what the tones in it should be) helps with identifying tonal features on machine--produced graphs, but the identification is possible, contrary to the current belief, without such help. And since the help comprises potentially misleading phonological assumptions, it is actually preferable to avoid it[4].

Rejection of the phonologically based shortcuts means, however, that a number of tedious questions have to be answered which would otherwise not even arise. One of these concerns distinguishing those bits of text (I use the term 'text' in a very loose meaning to refer to any continuous sample of real language) which are potential carriers of tone from those which are not. This applies both above and below the syllable borderline. On the one hand, one must find out which part of the syllable is relevant to tone perception (e.g. if the respective features of voiced consonant onsets contribute to it or not, etc.). On the other hand, it is necessary to investigate if all syllables are potential carriers of tone signals, and if this is not the case, how the carriers can be distinguished from the non-carriers. The experiment which will be described in this paper is concerned with one particular aspect of the latter. Its purpose is, roughly speaking, to attempt at establishing the minimum duration a Peking Dialect syllable presumably must have to act as tone carrier. In other words, it aims at delimiting, in the terms of syllable duration, those bits of text which must be taken into account as relevant to tone perception, as well as those which can be safely excluded.

The phonetic assumptions on which the experiment was necessarily based were deliberately restricted to the smallest possible number. It would not serve a useful purpose to present the case of each one in detail at this point (I am, of course, prepared to do so if requested to in discussion). The following statement summarizes all those which I am aware of.

Peking Dialect tone is reflected in the fundamental frequency, overall amplitude, and duration characteristics of a syllable. Only that part of the syllable which constitutes a clearly identifiable structure of harmonics is relevant in this respect. This includes the so-called nasal and retroflex codas but it excludes all onset features even though they may at times comprise brief bits of harmonic structure. The tone signal is perceived in the terms of deviation from mean values in the given frame of reference. Thus, it is of perceptual importance if the given syllable's overall F_0 and amplitude level is above or below that of syllables in its immediate environment, if its F_0 and overall amplitude contour has a peak in the beginning, in the middle, or at the end, and whether the peak deviates upwards or downwards of the rest of the contour, and, finally, if the syllable is shorter or longer than syllables around it. The deviation in the case of the F_0 and overall amplitude contour in particular requires a certain minimum amount of time to materialize and to be perceived. Duration thus must be relevant to delimiting the absolute threshold of tone perception, apart from its role in distinguishing tones from each other.

2. The Experiment

2.1. General Procedure

The experiment consisted of three stages. During the first stage, the average F_0, overall amplitude, and duration values of the four Peking Dialect tones were calculated on the basis of data obtained from a recorded dialogue. In the second stage, the average values were applied to the segmental base [pa] produced by a speech synthesizer. Each of the resulting four synthetic syllables was then stretched and contracted in duration, and also shifted up and down within the given range of F_0, so that in the end eighty syllable variants were synthesized. A tape was then prepared with these eighty syllables recorded in an entirely arbitrary order. In the last stage of the experiment, five speakers of Peking Dialect were asked to listen to the tape and try to indicate the tone of each syllable. Their responses were finally evaluated from the point of view of the degree to which the tones of the syllables were correctly recognized.

2.2. Stage 1

The data on which the experiment was based came from a commercially produced disc recording of a 相声 xiàngsheng dialogue with the title

相面 Xiàngmiàn 'Physiognomy', as performed by 侯宝林 Hóu Bǎolín

郭啟儒 Guō Qǐrú in Peking around 1965 (the disc was not dated). The speech of one of the two actors, Hóu Bǎolín, contained in the first five minutes of the dialogue (the actual time of Hóu Bǎolín's speech was 7.28 sec.) was copied onto tape and cut up into continuous bits of two seconds or less. For each of the bits several spectrograms of different type were made on a Model S Kay Sonagraph equipped with an amplitude display unit and a scale magnifier. The spectrograms were then analyzed in the following manner:

a. Each of the bits was segmented by using wide-band spectrograms, amplitude display sections, and the technique of partial erasure[5] as the main sources of evidence.

b. In each syllable obtained in the process of segmentation (a syllable being defined as a segment characterized by a homogeneous column of harmonics accompanied by an overall amplitude curve with a single peak directed upwards, and potentially containing a noise onset), the part constituting a structure of harmonics was divided into five equally wide vertical strips along the time scale (e.g. a column of harmonics lasting 50 msec. was divided into five 10 msec. strips). Six equally distant points were thus selected within each column of harmonics: one at its beginning, one at its end, and four in between at the border-lines of the strips.

c. At each of the six points along the given syllable's duration, measurements were made of F_0 and overall amplitude. F_0 was measured mainly from magnified spectrograms with the 200 c.p.s.-per-inch scale, and overall amplitude was measured from amplitude display sections[6].

All the syllables were then divided into five groups: one group (T5) contained syllables whose F_0 and overall amplitude characteristics could not be clearly associated with any of the four tones (these were mainly atonic syllables and what for the lack of a better term could be called intonation carriers, that is interjections and other similar items), and each of the other groups (T1-T4) consisted of syllables with the distinct characteristics of one of the four tones[7]. The total number of syllables classified in this manner was 461 (group T5 contained 137, T1 65, T2 88, T3 78, and T4 93, groups T1-T4 totalling 324 syllables).

Finally, the F_0, overall amplitude, and duration of all syllables within each of the groups T1-T4 were averaged by calculating their arithmetic mean. In the case of F_0 and overall amplitude, this was done for each of the six points separately, so that the result resembled a curve. The average values of the four tones arrived at in this manner are presented in Table 1.a. - d., with the six points numbered consecutively I - VI along the time scale. Group T5 was excluded from further consideration in the experiment.

2.3. Stage 2

The segmental base [pa] was selected as the most suitable carrier for the average values obtained in Stage 1. There were two main reasons for this choice. On the one hand, it is a very simple base which avoids such

10

problems as the effect of voiced consonant onsets, non-steady-state vowels, and nasal or retroflex codas on the three dimensions of tone. On the other hand, it is one of the very few bases of this kind which yield a free morpheme in conjunction with each of the four tones: [pa_] 'eight', [pa˩] 'to uproot', [pa˅] 'to hold', and [pa˯] 'dyke'. The latter aspect was of particular importance for the perceptual test to be carried out in Stage 3.

This segmental base was synthesized on the twelve-parameter electronic formant synthesizer controlled by a Honeywell DDP-224 on-line computer which is part of the speech synthesis facilities of the Bell Telephone Laboratories in Murray Hill, N. J.[8] The formant values for [a] were chosen as F1 1000 c.p.s., F2 1500 c.p.s., and F3 2460 c.p.s.[9] The consonant onset [p] was achieved by bending the formants towards the loci of 50 c.p.s. (for F1), 700 c.p.s. (for F2), and 2000 c.p.s. (for F3)[10], with full formant values of [a] reached 80 msec. from the loci. For further details on the synthesized segmental base see Appendix 1. Since all formant amplitudes had to be maintained at 0 during 0 - 20 msec. (i.e. for 20 msec. from the point of the loci) for the best results in synthesizing the consonant onset, a small amount of time was required for the segmental base to become sufficiently audible and thus able to carry tonal features. This was achieved at approximately 40 msec. from the loci, and that is where the first of the six points I - VI was placed. The synthesizer enabled changes in parameter values only every 10 msec., which meant that if the intervals between the six points were kept equal, the minimum duration of the tone-carrying part of the syllable was 50 msec., the next step was 100 msec., then 150 msec., and so on. The average duration calculated in Stage 1 had to be adapted to this. Therefore, the duration 100 msec. of the tone-carrying part of the syllable was selected for groups T1 (average duration 125 msec.), T2 (average duration 120 msec.), and T4 (average duration 120 msec.), and 150 msec. for T3 (average duration 145 msec.). For groups T1, T2, and T4, the timing of the six points was thus:

	(loci)	I	II	III	IV	V	VI
T1, T2, T4	0	40	60	80	100	120	140 msec.

For T3 it was:

	(loci)	I	II	III	IV	V	VI
T3	0	40	70	100	130	160	190 msec.

The average values which had been calculated for each tone were then applied to the segmental base in correspondence with this timing grid.

In the case of amplitude, the procedure was somewhat more complicated.

Firstly, the computer program which was used for synthesizing the base
did not require overall amplitude data but rather the values of the amplitude
of each of the three formants separately (as well as the amplitude of hiss
which did not come into account in this experiment) at any given point of
time. So as to make the average overall amplitude values calculated in
Stage 1 applicable, the proportion of 45 (amplitude of F1) : 45 (amplitude
of F2) : 10 (amplitude of F3) was chosen[11] for dividing them throughout.
Furthermore, the first five of the six points were timed in the same way
for amplitude as for F_o but no value was given for the point in time where
VI would be. The reason for this was that if all the amplitudes were defined
as 0 immediately after (i.e. 10 msec. after) a full value at VI to achieve
silence, the abrupt transition would cause an undesirable loud click re-
sembling a consonant coda. To avoid the click, a smoother transition to
silence was achieved by reducing all amplitudes to 0 at a point 10 msec.
after where VI would be, without actually giving any value there (i.e.
there was a direct transition to 0 from Point V which was at least 20 msec.
distant).

The result of applying F_o and amplitude values to the original segmental
base in the manner described above were four synthetic syllables [pa_],
[pa,], [pa⌄], and [pa.], which reflected, at least in the dimensions
assumed to be relevant to tone, the average features of tonal syllables
occurring in normal speech conditions. These four syllables were then
tampered with in two ways.

Firstly, each of the syllables was stretched and contracted by increasing
and reducing by 10 msec. the interval between the six points of its tone-
carrying part. The timing of the six points thus became

(loci)	I	II	III	IV	V	VI
Stretched T1, T2, T4	0	40	70	100	130	160	190 msec.
Stretched T3	0	40	80	120	160	200	240 msec.
Contracted T1, T2, T4	0	40	50	60	70	80	90 msec.
Contracted T3	0	40	60	80	100	120	140 msec.

One set A of stretched and contracted syllables were synthesized with
F_o and amplitude values remaining the same as in syllables with normal
duration: the curves were simply flattened out or bunched up. Since this
affected the actual shape of F_o and amplitude contours, another set B of
stretched and contracted syllables were prepared whose curves retained

the original shape by having the values proportionally modified[12]. The original group of four syllables thus became supplemented by eight stretched and eight contracted syllables (four in set A, and four in set B in either case). The obvious aim of preparing the sets of normal, stretched, and contracted variants was to investigate if the average syllable duration derived from real speech was sufficient for tone perception of the tone of isolated syllables, if perception improved with greater duration, and if it was affected by reducing duration below the level of average syllable duration in normal speech.

Secondly, every one of the twenty syllables synthesized so far was modified in its F_0 dimension by shifting its overall F_0 level up and down to match that of the corresponding syllables with the other three tones. A set of sixty syllables were thus added, the total number of synthesized syllables reaching eighty. The aim of preparing the last set was to investigate if overall F_0 level had anything to do with tone perception, and if its eventual contribution was related to syllable duration. It was assumed that any arrangement of the eighty syllables would provide a frame of F_0 level reference within which the listener would place the overall F_0 level of individual syllables.

The eighty syllables were selected and copied in random order from a tape prepared earlier on the Ampex AG-440 recorder which was part of the speech synthesis facility. They were then consecutively numbered and the numbers read in English were added to the copy of the tape preceding each given syllable. The order in which the syllables appeared on the tape is presented in Table 2. A test sheet was prepared for each informant undergoing the subsequent perceptual test, on which eighty consecutively numbered slots were matched with four Chinese characters representing the respective four morphemes (八 [pa_] 'eight', 拔 [pa˥] 'to uproot',

把 [pa˅] 'to hold', and 壩 [paˋ] 'dyke'). A question mark was

added as the fifth item to make it possible for the informants to indicate their inability to associate the given syllable with any of the four tones.

2.4.   Stage 3

Five speakers of Peking Dialect (for data on them see Appendix 2) were asked to take part in the perceptual test concluding the experiment. Four of them (A, B, C, and D) took the test together, the fifth (E) several days later separately, but conditions were otherwise identical for all five. After a brief introduction during which the informants were told what the nature of the taped material was, played a sample of it, and instructed how to

13

mark the test sheets (as it is perhaps obvious from the preceding section of this paper, they were asked to associate each syllable with either one of the four characters or the question mark by ticking it off on the sheet), the test tape was played once to them without interruption on a two-track Series 15 Tandberg tape recorder with a loudspeaker.

The informants' responses are presented in Tables 2-4. Table 2 is a list of the syllables and a transcript of the informants' marking arranged in the same order as the syllables appeared on the tape, and as the slots were numbered on the test sheet. Table 3 gives the marking arranged according to the individual tone groups. Finally, Table 4 summarizes the results for each of the four tone groups separately, and also for all four together.

2.5.   Notes on the results of the test

2.5.1. General remarks

On the whole, the informants responded very badly to the synthetic material: only 26 p.c. of the total number of syllables[13] were correctly identified (see Table 4.e.), and in the case of one of the four tonal groups (T3, see Table 4.c.), the experiment failed completely. This was perhaps partly due to the unusual nature of the material. None of the informants had heard synthetic speech before the test, and it was quite obvious that most of them were distracted by the novelty of the experience. However, it is likely that the main reason why the test showed such poor response was that items whose features had been derived from continuous speech were presented as isolated citation forms. This seemed to confuse the informants who all stated after the test that they missed features typical for tones pronounced in isolation, such as the characteristic dipping pitch contour of the low tone (T3), and, in particular, the usual long duration. It could be argued that presenting the syllables in isolation without providing them with the idiosyncratic features of isolated citation forms was a shortcoming of the test. However, this only emphasized the difference between citation forms and forms derived from normal speech, and it served as a strong indication that it is presumably an equal shortcoming to reverse the process and use isolated citation form syllables as the only or main source of data on tones. As is well known, this has been done in all the existing phonetic descriptions of Peking Dialect.

Proportional modification of the overall amplitude and F_o curves of stretched and contracted syllables appears to have had relatively little effect on tone perception. Syllables with modified curves did, however, give marginally better general results than those with flattened or bunched

14

up curves, and in a few isolated cases, curve modification seems to have made considerable difference (e.g. in stretched T1, see Table 3.a.).

Similarly, shifting the overall F_0 level up and down had surprisingly little influence on tone perception. In a few instances, shifting one of the high-level tones downwards to the level of T3 obviously confused the informants (e.g. in the case of stretched modified T1 lowered to T3 level, see Table 3.a.), and syllables whose F_0 was not shifted were generally responded to slightly better than the rest. However, there did not seem to be any clear relationship between shifting of this kind and different syllable duration: perception of all syllables tended to alter in much the same way by stretching and contraction. The lack of any considerable effect of overall F_0 level shifting on tone perception in the test was probably due to the failure of the informants in establishing a general frame of F_0 level reference for the whole set of eighty syllables. The informants presumably treated each syllable as an isolated item unrelated to the others in any respect (the fact that they were separated from each other by the English numbers may have contributed to this), and overall F_0 level thus did not seem to function as an important perception cue for them. As will be seen later, this was also the most likely reason why the experiment failed in the case of T3 syllables.

As for the main purpose of the experiment which was to investigate if and how syllable duration influenced tone perception, the test led to two important results. Firstly, it showed that tone perception generally improved with increased syllable duration, both in the sense that correct identification was more frequent, and that the number of 'don't know' responses decreased proportionally to the increase in duration. Secondly, the test made it clear that response to syllables whose tone-carrying part was 0.05 sec long (i.e. contracted T1, T2, and T4) was so erratic that their F_0 and amplitude contours could obviously not be perceived at all. These syllables were most likely perceived as contourless bursts of sound. It was probably because of this that there was a distinct trend in the test to interpret these syllables as T4: burst-like quality is a characteristic feature of syllables with this tone. In view of this, it can be proposed that tone distinctions in Peking Dialect fail to be perceived in the case of isolated syllables when their duration falls somewhere between 0.05 and 0.10 sec. This proposition is supported by the common observation of F_0 and overall amplitude contours in the acoustical analysis of syllables with duration around 0.05 sec. occurring in normal speech: these contours are usually so irregular that they cannot be clearly associated with tone characteristics. This does not necessarily mean that syllables of this or even shorter duration cannot be perceived as tonal in continuous speech, but it does imply that if they are, some features other than the F_0 and amplitude characteristics of the individual syllables themselves must serve as perception cues. One possible explanation is that tones of syllables with all durations are mostly perceived in normal speech not as individual items, but in the terms of tone configurations where identification is made by relating the tone components to each other rather than to an absolute frame of reference.

2.5.2. Group T1

Response to T1 syllables was relatively good (35 p.c. were recognized), and generally more consistent than to others. This may have been partly due to the fact that the token morpheme chosen to represent these syllables on the test sheet was 八 [pa_] 'eight' which is much more highly recurrent in Peking Dialect than the other three morphemes. It is rather interesting to note that 45 p.c. of all contracted T1 syllables were interpreted as T4, while not a single one was actually marked as T1. Syllable duration thus seemed to be of considerable importance for T1-T4 recognition.

Modified F_0 and amplitude curves yielded better results than the rest, especially in the case of stretched syllables. Distinct F_0 and amplitude contour thus appeared as equally important for T1 recognition.

Response to T1 was the weakest when the overall F_0 level was lowered to that characteristic for T3. This was one of the few instances in the test when overall F_0 level seemed of relevance for tone recognition.

The T1 group of syllables showed most convincingly the importance of duration for tone perception: no contracted T1 syllable was recognized but 40 p.c. of the normal duration group, and as many as 68 p.c. of the stretched group were correctly identified.

2.5.3. Group T2

Response to T2 syllables was moderately good (26 p.c. were recognized). 25 p.c. of contracted syllables in this group were again interpreted as T4 (cf. 2.5.2.).

In the case of T2 syllables, modified F_0 and amplitude curves produced better results than unmodified curves which showed a greater tendency towards being interpreted as T1 (especially when stretched). Distinct F_0 and amplitude contour thus seemed to be important for T2 recognition, similarly as in the case of T1.

Shifting the overall F_0 level had not much influence on T2 identification. When the level was raised to that of T4, informants were more inclined to interpret T2 as T1 (but not as T4 which perhaps indicates that T4 is mainly recognized by other features than overall F_0 level), and stretched T2 syllables lowered to T3 level surprisingly elicited very good response (70 p.c. were correctly recognized). However, it is quite possible that these were mere coincidences.

Duration was again of considerable importance for T2 identification. While contracted and normal T2 syllables yielded relatively poor response (17 p.c. and 15 p.c. were recognized), recognition improved greatly with stretched syllables (40 p.c.). The fact that slightly more of the contracted T2 syllables were recognized than those with normal duration was probably another coincidence. It could, however, mean that T2 syllables in isolation need a slightly longer duration than T1 syllables to be correctly identified.

2.5.4.   Group T3

As it was stated earlier, the test failed completely in the case of T3 syllables: only one of all the T3 syllables was recognized by one informant. It was suggested above that one of the reasons for this was that the T3 syllables used in the test lacked the idiosyncratic features of isolated T3 citation form syllables, namely the sharp rise of F_0 at the end, and abnormally long duration (the slightly greater duration of T3 syllables in comparison with all others in the test was obviously not quite sufficient). Apart from this, it must be pointed out that most of the T3 syllables in the test also lacked the low overall F_0 level characteristic for T3: since T1, T2, and T4 all deviate upwards within the F_0 range, all the overall F_0 level shifting of T3 syllables was upwards in different degrees. Nevertheless, even those T3 syllables whose F_0 level was not shifted were not correctly identified, which probably shows that the informants did not relate the syllables in the test to each other (see 2.5.1.). Disregarding the lacking citation form features, it thus appears that the main reason for the failure of the test in the case of T3 syllables was insufficient presence of the relative low overall F_0 level cue which is most likely of crucial importance for T3 recognition.

In view of this, it is not surprising that most T3 syllables were marked as T1. The curves of T1 and T3 are very similar in the sense that they have a centrally positioned deviation peak, and their main difference, the direction of the deviation, was practically obliterated by a lacking frame of F_0 reference. In comparison with true T1 syllables, the response to T3 as T1 was actually much better: 73 p.c. of T3 syllables were marked as T1, while only 35 p.c. of true T1 syllables were recognized. This was most likely due to the fact that the duration of T3 syllables used in the test was greater than that of T1 syllables, which eliminated from the T3 group the set equivalent to contracted T1 syllables.

It is of some interest to note that the response to T3 syllables could be said to follow the same general pattern as the response to all other syllables, if the recognition failure is disregarded (i.e. if marking T3 as T1 is accepted as correct identification).

2.5.5.   Group T4

Response to T4 syllables was the best within the test (41 p.c. were correctly identified), despite the fact that the morpheme chosen to represent the syllables on the test sheet was not very common (there are only two or three free morphemes sharing the syllable [pa、] in Peking Dialect, all of them rather uncommon).

Neither curve modification nor shifting the overall F_o level seemed to matter much in T4 recognition: T4 syllables with unmodified curves actually yielded slightly better results but shifting F_o level had the same relatively small effect as in the case of T1 and T2 syllables (i.e. recognition was slightly better in the case of syllables the F_o level of which had not been shifted).

However, what made this group different from all the rest was that the tendency towards greater degree of recognition with increased duration was much less pronounced: as many as 38 p.c. of contracted T4 syllables were correctly recognized, while only 40 p.c. of the normal duration set, and 45 p.c. of stretched T4 syllables were identified. Moreover, a very high proportion of contracted T1 and T2 syllables were marked as T4 (but not T3: there were no syllables of the very short 0.05 sec. duration in that group), as was pointed out earlier. It thus appears that short duration (that is, short within limits which did not become apparent during the experiment) and the resulting burst-like quality is what mainly characterizes T4 syllables in opposition to all other syllables in Peking Dialect. This conclusion is supported by the observation of the influence of stress on syllable duration in Peking Dialect: while stress prolongs T1, T2, and T3 syllables, it tends to shorten T4 syllables[14].

3. Conclusion

The experiment described in this paper showed that syllable duration
was highly relevant to tone perception in Peking Dialect, in the sense that
tones of most syllables with relatively long duration were more easily
perceived than those of shorter syllables. The absolute threshold for
perceiving tones of individual syllables appeared to be between 0.05 and
0.10 sec.: F_0 and overall amplitude characteristics of individual syllables
whose duration fell below this threshold were not sufficient for correct
tone recognition. Syllables with the falling tone (T4) were an exception
in this respect. Their tone perception threshold seemed to be lower than
that of the syllables with other tones but the experiment did not reveal
how much lower it actually was.

The conclusion about the tone perception threshold is quite startling if
it is taken into account that almost one half of all syllables occurring
in normal speech in Peking Dialect usually have tone-carrying parts of
less than 0.10 sec. in duration: with the exclusion of T4 syllables, the
section of the dialogue which was used in Stage 1 of the experiment contained 44 p.c. of syllables whose duration was between 0.05 and 0.10 sec.
One might conclude on the basis of this that Peking Dialect is not a fully
tonal language but perhaps a more plausible conclusion is that tones are
not identified individually for each syllable in normal speech but, as it
was suggested earlier, that they are rather perceived in configurations
or clusters. Each configuration as a whole presumably contains perception
cues which are not part of any of the component syllables' F_0 and overall
amplitude buildup. It should be pointed out here that very little has been
done so far in Chinese phonetics in the area of tone configurations: with
the exception of some studies of groups of two or more tones[15] (all of
which, however, approached the issue in the terms of combinations or
rather sequences of individual tones rather than distinct complex units),
most phonetic descriptions of Peking Dialect tones have been concerned
with tones in isolation.

The experiment further showed that overall F_0 level had little effect on
the perception of the tones of individual syllables. However, it was
designed in such a way that it could not reveal whether this was equally
true for tone configurations in normal speech. It would seem most unlikely
that this would actually be the case. The failure of the experiment in the
case of T3 syllables indicated the importance of relative F_0 level for tone
perception in normal speech conditions.

Apart from these conclusions, it is possible to find support in the test
part of the experiment in particular, for the view that tone is phonetically
a three-dimensional complex with neither dimension of clear perceptual

predominance at all times and in all circumstances. It was, for example, shown that while the shape of F_o and overall amplitude contour was very important for the recognition of some tones (T1 and T2), it was less important for the perception of the falling tone (T4) where syllable duration was of greater relevance, etc. This implies that it is misleading to consider pitch as the exclusive or generally predominant phonetic dimension of tones in Peking Dialect, however convenient this may be from the point of view of phonology.

Finally, the experiment indirectly emphasized the special nature of the tone variants which occur in isolated citation form syllables. These variants which could perhaps be best treated as traditional Chinese labels for the four tones rather than target value manifestations, seem to be of little importance for the study of tones in normal Peking Dialect speech. It is rather unfortunate that they have been commonly used in Chinese phonetics as the starting point for the analysis of tones, and that their idiosyncratic features have become considered as general tone characteristics.

NOTES

1   For a general linguistic source see Pike, p. 9. Chao's Grammar,
     p. 25 ff., is the most representative for the traditional Chinese
     linguistic approach. Ideologically more up to date but hardly any
     more enlightening phonetically is Wang, p. 96 ff. Even many fairly
     recent works using acoustic data, e.g. Brotzman, and describing
     perception experiments, such as Li, assume that pitch is the sole
     dimension of tone.

2.   Hockett, pp. 256-7, was perhaps the first linguist to say that 'the
     tones are contrasting contours of pitch, volume, glottalization, and
     length', but he did not elaborate beyond a few brief and impressionis-
     tic statements. Švarný and Spešnev, among others, were phonetically
     more explicit, despite their instrumental limitations.

3   See Noll, pp. 293-4.

4   This does not imply that it is possible to derive the tonal structure
     of a text merely from phonetic measurements. All it proposes is the
     possibility to identify those phonetic features which are perceptible
     (rather than perceived) and interpretable (rather than interpreted) as
     tones, and separate them from those which are not. The underlying
     suggestion is that this kind of identification would be more valuable
     than the customary application of phonological shortcuts.

5   This technique is based on controlled gradual erasure of small sec-
     tions of the copy recorded on the flywheel of the Sonagraph, with
     reference to the corresponding wide-band spectrogram, and compa-
     rison of the original recording with the partly erased copy by ear.
     To make this possible, a push-on switch connected to the erase head
     was added to the control panel of the Sonagraph (at the Department of
     Linguistics, University of Cambridge), and a pointer was mounted
     next to the cylinder which matched the position of the erase head
     with the corresponding part of the spectrogram wound around the
     cylinder.

6   For the sake of simplicity, arbitrary linear units of length (1/20
     inch equalling 10 units) were used for measuring overall amplitude
     from amplitude display sections made with the narrow-band filter,
     taking the section baseline as 0. These units happened to be very
     easily translatable into the kind of instructions required for defining
     amplitude values by the computer program used in Stage 2 (also see
     Appendix 1, parameters A1, A2, A3, and HA).

7   A certain amount of cheating took place here. Admittedly, one did not always place such syllables as [wuoˇ] (wǒ 'I') into Group T3, etc., only and strictly because of what they looked like on spectrograms. However, in a few cases when a syllable expected to belong to one of the tone groups looked strikingly different from other syllables in the group, it was placed in Group T5.

8   I should like to experess my deep gratitude to the Bell Telephone Laboratories for their generosity in letting me use their synthesizer and other equipment during January–October 1969. Special thanks must be directed to Dr. P.B. Denes for his kind help and patience with a technically ignorant sinologue. The speech synthesis facility in question is described in a number of papers, e.g. Jensen, most of which have not, unfortunately, been published. For a description of an earlier version of the facility see Coker and Cummiskey.

9   I greatly profited from the opportunity to make use of the extensive vowel formant measurements made by John M. Howie of the University of Missouri in the preparation of his Ph. D. dissertation. I am most grateful to him for letting me have a copy of large parts of his manuscript.

10   Cf. Delattre, pp. 201 and 208–9.

11   This appeared to be the most acceptable formant amplitude proportion common to Peking Dialect oral vowels as synthesized on the facility referred to earlier. It was arrived at by trial and error rather than on the basis of acoustic measurements.

12   The modification was made by using overall F_0 level as the basis from which the relative distance of the individual values was proportionally adjusted. Overall F_0 level was calculated here and elsewhere in the experiment as the arithmetic mean of the values at points I – VI.

13   In statements giving percentages the 'total number of syllables' (i.e. 100 p.c.) refers to all instances in which the given syllables were responded to by individual informants. Thus, the total number of syllables used in the whole test is considered as 400 (the set of eighty syllables each of which was responded to five times) for this purpose.

14   See Kratochvil, p. 159.

15   See Li and Dreher, Young, and Lee.

REFERENCES

Brotzman, R. 'Progress Report on Mandarin Tone Study', POLA Report No. 8, The Ohio State University, 1964, 1-35.

Chao, Y.R. A Grammar of Spoken Chinese, Berkeley and Los Angeles, 1968.

Coker, C.H., and Cummiskey, P. 'On-line Computer Control of a Formant Synthesizer', The Journal of the Acoustical Society of America, 38 (1965), 940 (A).

Delattre, P. 'From Acoustic Cues to Distinctive Features', Phonetica, 18 (1968), 198-230.

Dreher, J.J., Young, E.L., and Lee, P.C. Mandarin Triplet Contours, Research Communication 107, Douglas Advanced Research Laboratories, Huntington Beach, Cal., 1969.

Hockett, C.F. 'Peiping Phonology'. Journal of the American Oriental Society, 67 (1947), 253-267.

Howie, J.M. The Vowels and Tones of Mandarin Chinese: Acoustical Measurements and Experiments, unpublished Ph.D. dissertation, University of Missouri, 1970.

Jensen, O.C. Capabilities of the DDP-224 On-line Computer, unpublished, 1968.

Kratochvil, P. 'On the Phonology of Peking Stress', Transactions of the Philological Society, 1967, 154-178.

Li, K.P. 'Tone Perception Experiment', POLA Report No. 6r, The Ohio State University, 1963, 19-26.

Noll, A.M. 'Cepstrum Pitch Determination', The Journal of the Acoustical Society of America, 41 (1967), 293-309.

Pike, K.L. Tone Languages, Ann Arbor, 1956.

Spešnev, N.A. 'Akustičeskaja priroda slovesnogo udarenija v sovremennom kitajskom jazyke' ('The Acoustic Nature of Word Stress in Contemporary Chinese'), Voprosy korejskogo i kitajskogo jazykoznanija, Leningrad, 1958, 138-149.

Švarný, O. Prosodické vlastnosti slabiky v čínštině a jejich modifikace v řeči mluvené (The Prosodic Properties of the Syllable in Chinese and Their Modification in Continuous Speech), unpublished dissertation, Prague, 1952.

Wang, W. S-Y. 'Phonological Features of Tone', International Journal of American Linguistics, 33 (1967), 93-105.

APPENDIX 1

Description of the segmental base [pa] as synthesized on the formant
synthesizer controlled by the Honeywell DDP-224 computer.

F_o: 0/180, [Point I] - [Point VI], [Point VI] + 10/200

F1:   0/50, 80/1000 ...

F2:   0/700, 80/1500 ...

F3:   0/2000, 80/2460 ...

B1:   0/100 ...

B2:   0/30, 30/80 ...

A1:
A2: }   0/0, 20/0, [Point I] - [Point V], [Point VI] + 10/0
A3:

HF: 0/2000 ...

HA: 0/0 ...

BH: 0/0, 30/10, 40/100 ...

Note.

Of the twelve parameters above, F_o is fundamental frequency in c.p.s.
F1, F2, and F3 are formant frequencies of the three formants in c.p.s.
B1 is the bandwidth of the first formant, B2 of the second and third
formants, both in c.p.s. A1, A2, and A3 are amplitudes of the three
formants in units ranging from 0 (silence) to 100 (maximum loudness).
HF is the center frequency of hiss in c.p.s. HA is the amplitude of hiss
in the same units as A1, A2, and A3. BH is the so-called buzz-hiss proportion in units ranging from 0 (all hiss) to 100 (all buzz). The number
to the left of the slash gives time in msec., the number to the right of the
slash is the value in the given units. Three dots indicate that the last value
is maintained to the end of the syllable. In the case of F_o, A1, A2, and A3
values presented in Table 1 have to be inserted according to the timing
grids described in Section 2.3. of the paper. The values 180 c.p.s. at 0
msec., and 200 c.p.s. at [Point VI] + 10 msec. in the F_o parameter are
terminal values shared by all four tones. They were added to provide the
increasing and decreasing amplitudes with F_o values at the edges of the
contours, and although they are in correspondence with the tendencies of
all four F_o contours, their contribution to their shape was negligible. The
value 2000 c.p.s. in the HF parameter is a dummy value.

APPENDIX 2

Informants

All the informants were professional teachers of Chinese living in England at the time of the test, and they all had university background.

Informant A was a man, born in Hong Kong in 1929. His father was a
high government official, both parents came from Canton. He was educated
in Modern Standard Chinese and lived in various parts of China until his
departure for England in 1949. His wife was English. He spoke good
acquired Peking Dialect.

B was also a man, born in Peking in 1911. His father was an intellectual,
originally from Southwestern China, mother came from Central China,
but both parents spoke acquired Peking Dialect. He lived mainly in Peking
until 1949 when he first moved to Hong Kong, and later to England. He
was not married, and he was a native speaker of Peking Dialect.

C was a man, born in Peking in 1916. His father was a businessman, both
parents came from Peking. He lived in Peking until the Sino-Japanese War
when he moved to Southwestern China. He stayed in Hong Kong from 1949
until 1966 when he came to England. His wife was from Shantung. He was
a native speaker of Peking Dialect.

D was a woman, born in Peking in 1925. Her father was a civil servant,
both parents came from Peking. She lived in Peking until 1948, then stayed
in Hong Kong until 1966 when she came to England. She was not married,
and she was a native speaker of Peking Dialect.

E was a man, born in Kansu in 1925. His father was a civil servant, both
parents came from Northwestern China. He was educated in Modern Standard Chinese, and lived mainly in Northern China until his departure for
Taiwan in 1948. He came to England in 1967. His wife was from Hupeh.
He spoke good acquired Peking Dialect.

TABLE 1

Average F_O, overall amplitude, and duration values of the analyzed syllable

a. The high tone (T1)

Points:	I	II	III	IV	V	VI	
F_O	0/210	25/230	50/245	75/245	100/235	125/220	msec./c.p.s
A	0/65	25/120	50/145	75/145	100/135	125/110*	msec./A un
							(see Note 6)

Overall duration: 125 msec. Overall F_O level: 230 c.p.s. *Omitted in synth

b. The rising tone (T2)

Points:	I	II	III	IV	V	VI	
F_O	0/195	24/205	48/215	72/225	96/230	120/225	msec./c.p.s
A	0/65	24/110	48/130	72/140	96/140	120/115*	msec./A un
							(see Note 6)

Overall duration: 120 msec. Overall F_O level: 215 c.p.s. *Omitted in synth

c. The low tone (T3)

Points:	I	II	III	IV	V	VI	
F_O	0/180	29/175	58/175	87/180	116/180	145/185	msec./c.p.s
A	0/60	29/115	58/120	87/120	116/115	145/110*	msec./A un
							(see Note 6)

Overall duration: 145 msec. Overall F_O level: 180 c.p.s. *Omitted in synth

d. The falling tone (T4)

Points:	I	II	III	IV	V	VI	
F_O	0/240	24/255	48/255	72/245	96/230	120/210	msec./c.p.s
A	0/70	24/140	48/150	72/130	96/115	120/100*	msec./A un
							(see Note 6)

Overall duration: 120 msec. Overall F_O level: 240 c.p.s. *Omitted in synth

TABLE 2

List of the 80 synthetic syllables and the informants' interpretation of them

	A	B	C	D	E			A	B	C	D	E
1. 1(4)NU	?	1	1	1	1		41. 3(2)NU	1	1	1	1	1
2. 2(2)SU	1	2	2	1	2		42. 1(1)CU	?	2	?	4	?
3. 2(4)SM	1	1	2	1	1		43. 4(1)SM	?	4	1	1	4
4. 3(2)SU	1	4	?	1	1		44. 1(3)SU	?	2	2	1	?
5. 4(4)NU	?	4	?	4	4		45. 3(4)CU	?	1	1	1	1
6. 3(1)CU	?	1	?	1	1		46. 1(2)CM	?	2	?	4	?
7. 1(1)SM	1	1	1	1	1		47. 2(4)CU	?	2	?	1	?
8. 4(1)SU	?	4	1	4	1		48. 1(1)NU	?	4	?	1	?
9. 1(3)CU	4	4	?	4	?		49. 3(2)CM	?	2	2	2	1
10. 4(2)NU	?	4	1	1	4		50. 2(3)SU	?	2	2	1	2
11. 2(1)SM	1	2	2	1	1		51. 3(3)CU	?	?	?	1	1
12. 2(2)NU	1	1	2	1	1		52. 4(2)SU	?	4	?	4	?
13. 1(2)CU	4	4	?	4	?		53. 2(3)SM	?	2	2	2	2
14. 3(4)CM	?	1	?	1	1		54. 3(3)SU	1	1	1	1	1
15. 2(2)CM	4	4	?	4	?		55. 4(3)NU	?	2	?	4	4
16. 3(3)SM	1	1	?	2	2		56. 3(1)CM	1	1	1	1	1
17. 2(3)CU	?	4	?	4	?		57. 1(4)CU	?	2	?	4	?
18. 1(4)SU	1	1	1	1	1		58. 2(1)SU	1	2	1	1	?
19. 2(2)CU	?	4	?	4	2		59. 4(3)SM	4	4	4	4	?
20. 3(2)CU	?	1	1	1	1		60. 3(2)SM	1	1	1	1	1
21. 1(3)SM	?	3	?	2	2		61. 1(3)CM	?	4	4	4	2
22. 4(3)CU	?	2	4	4	?		62. 2(4)SU	1	1	1	1	1
23. 1(2)SM	1	1	1	1	1		63. 2(1)NU	?	2	?	1	1
24. 4(2)CM	?	2	4	4	?		64. 3(4)SU	1	1	1	1	1
25. 3(3)CM	?	2	3	1	2		65. 2(1)CU	?	2	2	2	?
26. 4(1)CU	?	4	?	4	?		66. 3(1)NU	1	1	1	1	1
27. 4(4)SU	4	1	4	1	4		67. 2(2)SM	?	2	1	2	?
28. 3(1)SM	1	1	1	1	1		68. 4(1)CM	?	1	?	4	?
29. 2(4)CM	?	2	?	4	1		69. 4(4)SM	?	1	1	1	1
30. 2(1)CM	?	2	?	4	?		70. 1(2)NU	?	1	?	1	?
31. 1(1)CM	?	2	?	4	4		71. 4(2)CU	?	2	1	4	?
32. 2(3)CM	?	3	?	4	?		72. 1(1)SU	?	1	1	1	1
33. 3(4)SM	1	1	1	1	1		73. 4(4)CM	?	4	?	4	?
34. 1(2)SU	4	2	?	1	1		74. 2(4)NU	?	1	1	1	1
35. 3(1)SU	1	1	1	1	1		75. 1(4)SM	1	1	1	1	1
36. 4(2)SM	?	4	?	4	4		76. 4(4)CU	?	4	4	4	?
37. 3(3)NU	?	1	?	1	?		77. 3(4)NU	1	1	2	1	1
38. 4(3)SU	?	2	?	4	4		78. 4(1)NU	?	2	?	1	4
39. 1(4)CM	?	4	4	4	4		79. 1(3)NU	?	?	2	1	2
40. 4(3)CM	?	2	4	4	?		80. 2(3)NU	?	?	?	1	2

Note.

The first number after each period indicates the tone contour of the given syllable. The number in parentheses following it states the overall F_o level adopted for the given tone contour. For example, 1(4) means 'the syllable has the F_o and overall amplitude contour of the high tone (T1), and its overall F_o level is raised to that of the falling tone (T4)'. The following letter symbols indicate that the given syllable has either the duration normal for the given tonal group (N), or contracted duration (C), or stretched duration (S), and that its F_o and amplitude values either remained unmodified (U) or were modified (M) when it was stretched and contracted. The five interpretation columns are labelled A-E, each column representing the response of one informant.

TABLE 3

The informants' responses arranged according to tone groups.

a. The high tone (T1):

	A	B	C	D	E
1(1)NU	?	4	?	1	?
1(1)CU	?	2	?	4	?
1(1)SU	?	1	1	1	1
1(1)CM	?	2	?	4	4
1(1)SM	1	1	1	1	1
1(2)NU	?	1	?	1	?
1(2)CU	4	4	?	4	?
1(2)SU	4	2	?	1	1
1(2)CM	?	2	?	4	?
1(2)SM	1	1	1	1	1
1(3)NU	?	?	2	1	2
1(3)CU	4	4	?	4	?
1(3)SU	?	2	2	1	?
1(3)CM	?	4	4	4	2
1(3)SM	?	3	?	2	2
1(4)NU	?	1	1	1	1
1(4) CU	?	2	?	4	2
1(4)SU	1	1	1	1	1
1(4)CM	?	4	4	4	4
1(4)SM	1	1	1	1	1

b. The rising tone (T2):

	A	B	C	D	E
2(2)NU	1	1	2	1	1
2(2)CU	?	4	?	4	2
2(2)SU	1	2	2	1	2
2(2)CM	4	4	?	4	?
2(2)SM	?	2	1	2	?
2(1)NU	?	2	?	1	1
2(1)CU	?	2	2	2	?
2(1)SU	1	2	1	1	?
2(1)CM	?	2	?	4	?
2(1)SM	1	2	2	1	1
2(3)NU	?	?	?	1	2
2(3)CU	?	4	?	4	?
2(3)SU	?	2	2	1	2
2(3)CM	?	3	?	4	?
2(3)SM	?	2	2	2	2
2(4)NU	?	1	1	1	1
2(4)CU	?	2	?	1	?
2(4)SU	1	1	1	1	1
2(4)CM	?	2	?	4	1
2(4)SM	1	1	2	1	1

c. The low tone (T3):

	A	B	C	D	E
3(3)NU	?	1	?	1	?
3(3)CU	?	?	?	1	1
3(3)SU	1	1	1	1	1
3(3)CM	?	2	3	1	2
3(3)SM	1	1	?	2	2
3(1)NU	1	1	1	1	1
3(1)CU	?	1	?	1	1
3(1)SU	1	1	1	1	1
3(1)CM	1	1	1	1	1
3(1)SM	1	1	1	1	1
3(2)NU	1	1	1	1	1
3(2)CU	?	1	1	1	1
3(2)SU	1	4	?	1	1
3(2)CM	?	2	2	2	1
3(2)SM	1	1	1	1	1
3(4)NU	1	1	2	1	1
3(4)CU	?	1	1	1	1
3(4)SU	1	1	1	1	1
3(4)CM	?	1	?	1	1
3(4)SM	1	1	1	1	1

d. The falling tone (T4):

	A	B	C	D	E
4(4)NU	?	4	?	4	4
4(4)CU	?	4	4	4	?
4(4)SU	4	1	4	1	4
4(4)CM	?	4	?	4	?
4(4)SM	?	1	1	1	1
4(1)NU	?	2	?	1	4
4(1)CU	?	4	?	4	?
4(1)SU	?	4	1	4	1
4(1)CM	?	1	?	4	?
4(1)SM	?	4	1	1	4
4(2)NU	?	4	1	1	4
4(2)CU	?	2	1	4	?
4(2)SU	?	4	?	4	?
4(2)CM	?	2	4	4	?
4(2)SM	?	4	?	4	4
4(3)NU	?	2	?	4	4
4(3)CU	?	2	4	4	?
4(3)SU	?	2	?	4	4
4(3)CM	?	2	4	4	?
4(3)SM	4	4	4	4	?

Note. For explanation of numbers and ltters symbols see TABLE 2.

TABLE 4

Summary of the informants' responses in p.c.

a. The high tone (T1)

	Correctly identified	T2	T3	T4	?
			Interpreted as		
Total	35	12	1	20	32
Unmodified curves	33	12	0	17	38
Modified curves	38	12	2	25	23
Not shifted F_0 level	40	8	0	16	36
Shifted F_0 level	33	13	1	22	31
Contracted	0	12	0	45	43
Normal duration	40	10	0	5	45
Stretched	68	13	2	2	15

b. The rising tone (T2)

	Correctly identified	T1	T3	T4	?
			Interpreted as		
Total	26	32	1	10	31
Unmodified curves	25	38	0	7	30
Modified curves	28	22	2	15	33
Not shifted F_0 level	28	28	0	20	24
Shifted F_0 level	25	33	2	7	33
Contracted	17	5	3	25	50
Normal duration	15	55	0	0	30
Stretched	40	47	0	0	13

c. The low tone (T3)

	Correctly identified	Interpreted as			
		T1	T2	T4	?
Total	1	74	8	1	16
Unmodified curves	0	78	2	2	18
Modified curves	2	68	18	0	12
Not shifted F_0 level	4	48	16	0	32
Shifted F_0 level	0	83	5	1	11
Contracted	2	58	13	0	27
Normal duration	0	80	5	0	15
Stretched	0	88	5	2	5

d. The falling tone (T4)

	Correctly identified	Interpreted as			
		T1	T2	T3	?
Total	41	15	7	0	37
Unmodified curves	42	13	8	0	37
Modified curves	40	18	5	0	37
Not shifted F_0 level	44	24	0	0	32
Shifted F_0 level	40	12	9	0	39
Contracted	38	5	10	0	47
Normal duration	40	15	10	0	35
Stretched	45	25	2	0	28

e. All syllables

	Correctly identified	Interpreted as Different tones	?
Total	26	45	29
Unmodified curves	25	44	31
Modified curves	27	47	26
Not shifted F_0 level	29	40	31
Shifted F_0 level	25	47	28
Contracted	14	44	42
Normal duration	24	45	31
Stretched	38	47	15

DISCUSSION ON KRATOCHVIL'S PAPER: AN EXPERIMENT IN THE PERCEPTION OF PEKING DIALECT TONES.

Malmqvist: Would it be possible to include a fourth dimension. I am referring to the tonally conditioned distribution of articulatory force throughout the syllable. There is a correlation which is very clearly observable to the ear, that is between crescendo distributional articulatory force and rising pitch, and diminuendo and falling tone. In Szuch'uanese there is a very clearcut correlation between the intrasyllabic distribution of duration and this volume of stress manifestation. You have a progressive intrasyllabic distribution of duration.

Kratochvil: I am not quite clear about what you mean by the fourth dimension. There could be two things involved in this. One of them, in acoustic terms, would be overall amplitude, i.e. loudness contour. That contour was, in fact, taken into account here: it was one of the aspects of the material used in the experiment that the synthetic syllables did not differ from each other only in the pitch contour but also in the loudness contour. In the case of the 1st and the 3rd tone, the loudness contour had a centrally positioned peak, while in the case of the 2nd and the 4th tone the loudness contour more or less followed the respective pitch contour. There is, however, one other consideration involved here, and this was one of the reasons why I chose the syllable [pa] rather than any other. This syllable happens to avoid the problem of the proportional duration of the individual subcomponent within the syllables' tone-carrying components. Let's say, for instance, the relative duration of diphthong components which will presumably vary slightly according to the tone of the syllable in question.

Malmqvist: You will have a lengthening of a nasal final in the rising tone and a shortening in the falling tone. Those manifestations are very strong in whispered speech.

Kratochvil: I think your remark on whispered speech is most interesting. More analytical work should be done in this area. So far, all the experiments with whispered speech have suffered from the effects of the tone-equals-pitch fallacy. Perhaps one of the reasons why there has been this very strong tendency towards assuming that tones were exclusively pitch features, is that it is extremely difficult, using normal speech and the present-day technical equipment, to experiment with anything but changes in fundamental frequency. I think the machine most responsible for this is the tape-recorder which tends to compress the amplitude contour into a very narrow range, thus all but eliminating the subtle ups and downs in the loudness of recorded speech. This makes, in my opinion, taped material virtually useless for perceptual experiments involving some amplitude considerations. Nowadays, if you want to carry out an experiment, using normal speech, directed towards the problem of how tones are operated with in whispered speech, you either use live speakers or tape recordings in your perceptual tests. In the case of tape recordings you will probably reduce all the discernible dimensions to fundamental frequency and duration, so that features of any other dimension which might take over tone recognition will not be identified. In the case of live speakers you will get such inconsistency in performance that any semblance of control over the experiment will disappear.

Malmqvist: I have no experience whatsoever of mechanical tone perception but it would seem to me that there could be three factors influencing the selec tion of response. You mentioned one of them, i.e. the frequency of occurrence of the morpheme. Obviously a more frequent morpheme will occur more frequently in the responses. Secondly I think that the number of homophones would influence it too. The larger the number the less the likelyhood of having a poor response. And thirdly I think that the free versus bound status of the morpheme would influence it.

Kratochvil: The informants were, in fact, choosing between four characters, and the question mark was added as the fifth choice for the case when they simply could not identify the given syllable with any of the four characters.

Malmqvist: You would have got a much poorer result if you had not identified the forms.

Kratochvil: I am sure of that.

Rygaloff: I am wondering if the case of Pekingese is not a particularly unfavourable one because as we all know the prosody of Pekingese is a very complicated one with stress playing a very important part, and the context having to be considered in most cases. If you take a syllable out of context it is not possible to identify it. I wonder what the result would be in a case like Cantonese where there is practically no stress. Sandhi is unknown in Cantonese which means that every syllable is supposed to be realized in such a way that it has to be recognized. It seems to me that the case of Pekingese is marginal in the whole dialect complex of Chinese.

Kratochvil: Experiments of this kind have not yet been carried out for other dialects, unfortunately. Presumably, the physiological mechanism which is involved in tone perception is the same for all Chinese dialects. If it is true that Peking Dialect is marginal in the sense that the tonal features of individual syllables are more than usually modified by non-tonal phenomena, then it is a difficult test case, and therefore a good test case.

Egerod: I had the feeling that it is from a certain point of view not correct to say that Peking is marginal. I have tried to make a study of the history of tones in terms of original phonation types and it seems to me that Peking is one of those dialects which from the historical point of view is closer to the more varied origin of tones than what we find in Cantonese. I would say that Cantonese is sort of the end-point of an evolution and interesting in the fact that from all of these points of view it is so close to Thai. At least standard Thai and several of the Thai dialects spoken close to Chinese have tones which are pretty much distinguishable only by means of pitch whereas Peking, as said, shows this very different kind of problems. It seems to me that it is perhaps not right to call them marginal as they are present over such a large area and as those dialects, which do not have them, from my point of view would be marginal because those are the ones which typologically go with the neighbouring languages.

Rygaloff: I am saying marginal because of the fact that Pekingese has no ju sheng and it is the only area where it has been lost. Even if you consider ju sheng as something outside the tonal system it does play an important part in the interpretation of the syllabic forms. This may be one of the reasons why Pekingese has developed such a strong system of stress. In the case of Cantonese the tone-system is two-dimensional and supposed to consist of pitch and length. Only pitch difference appear in ju sheng. Very likely the Cantonese system is also over-simplified by phonologists but I still think that you cannot just throw away phonological considerations.

Kratochvil: I was not trying to throw out phonological considerations. Of course phonology must simplify. However what I was trying to say was that the simplification which is based on phonological considerations has no place in phonetics. What happens is that the phonologist is looking for the one feature which is of overall importance for the distinguishing of a whole set of phenomena and when he finds it he then operates in its terms.

Egerod: This objection which is very important to you as a phonetician is as important to the rest of us for historical reasons. We need these so called redundant features.

Egerod: There are so many points one could raise from this discussion. My first reaction would be, what are we testing? Are we testing the machine or the informants? The results are bad, so the machine is bad, or what they were given was no good. Because what you are doing is to willfully distort something and see whether it is still any good. To what extent have you tried to do it as well as possible? To what extent have you tried to make tones so that they can really be distinguished and then get the best results you could possibly get? Has this been part of it?

Kratochvil: It has not been the aim of this particular experiment, I am sure it is very important.

Egerod: I mean that it is an important part of this experiment because it seems to me that it is hard to test the validity of distortions if you do not know distortions from what. I would like to see all this in relation to: now we try as we best can to make a third tone so that an informant will imme- diately say, this is "pa$_v$". Against this we test all kinds of other things and then we will see how the accuracy gradually drops. I mean, is the machine any good at all. We have to be able to compare it with something that is valid. I am at least to a certain extent left with too many interferencies, most of them which you have brought up yourself. Certainly this experiment indicates something, but are we quite sure what it is. I think the conclusion has to be tested against some standard so that we can see what we really are testing. On this basis I am of course terribly interested in the whole thing, because I am trying to put "redundant" features in a historical re- lationship and to see what they might teach us about reconstructions. Any- thing that you find to play down the role of pitch is so much the better be- cause so much more important must those other features be that we can use for historical purposes.

Some other points. You say that it is on phonological grounds that people get the idea of overdoing the pitch part of it. But this certainly precedes what we call phonology. It must be something which has also caused phono- logy itself to come up. Certainly, long before people thought of doing anything like making a phonemic analysis, did you have people think that pitch was the valid thing in Chinese. Actually you will have people who have never heard of phonetics, who have never heard of phonology, who have never heard of history of linguistics, who would tell you the same thing. So if it is wrong, then it is either the result of something that has also played a role in building up phonology, or it has to do with the original speech of those people who were investigated. It is not terribly likely be- cause this mistake, if it is a mistake, has been made by Portuguese, Swedes and Danes and so on, and I do not know what it is they have in common in this aspect. But I just want to say that it is certainly not phono- logical theory, so there must be some other reason.

I find it very paradoxical to see your stressing that you can identify tonal features on machine-producing graphs. The identification is possible without any recourse to meaning, if I understand you right. It is wonderful to see this come up just at the time in the history of linguistics when the attempt to do this has finally been given up. And now the machine has become so good that we can do without meaning. To me it must be one of the great paradoxes in the history of linguistics.

You tell us how much of the syllable you include and that you exclude onset features. You might of course be excluding something which is relevant and certainly the active glottal onset is more common with 1st tone than with 2nd tone. It must be relevant somehow. I mean we know it is historically relevant, but it is probably also relevant for the perception of the 2nd tone. It should be tested again what people do if they get that. Is it easier to recognize a_-a, if you have that onset than if you do not have it? Otherwise you do not quite know what it is you compare with.

And then there is the whole aim of delimiting the absolute threshold of tone perception in terms of duration. You have a lot of informants. They have varied backgrounds and their ability to perceive tones without the correct duration may be very different. It would be interesting to see whether there is any correlation between their linguistic background and their ability to do this. If they also happen to know another dialect where this plays no role or where it plays a greater role it would necessarily have some kind of influence. Again, we need correctional tests that would give us the clue to what the conclusions of these important indications are.

We have already mentioned the relative frequency of the words that you test. It seems to me that if you in isolation hear something that sounds like "pa_" in Chinese and you have nothing to compare it with, it is out of context, you immediately think of "eight" even if it is slightly wrong, and the more since what these people hear is something that sounds like a funny machine that does not quite know how to say "eight" rather than a machine trying to say something else. Perhaps it only tells us that "eight" is a more common word in Chinese than "to uproot". If it tells us more it has to be tested against something, because that would be the first conclusion that we would reach, and that would not be so important as some other conclusions that we might want.

I would also stress the point which Malmqvist made about varying stress within the syllable varying amplitude. This again cannot come out in the clipped ones so you have from the beginning excluded yourself from giving the person the thing which he perhaps is primarily looking for. And then it is not strange that he does not hear that thing when he has to listen for a secondary thing. But you then conclude, it is not pitch so then it is duration because that is what I have taken out. But when you have also taken other things out like the different types of onsets and the different kinds of glottal friction in the middle of the tone and things like that, and they also are not as perceptible as you are used to, how do you know that it is duration that is the decisive factor here. I think one can find out, and you are probably going to find out, by tests where you do put in these other things and take out the other things, but till that has been done, I do not think that we can be sure that it is really duration that you are talking about.

I think one has to be a little careful about the conclusions concerning the 4th tone. You say that since they get it right because you have taken out duration, or you have altered the duration in these different tones and since they get the 4th tone right anyhow, it must mean that duration plays a role. But is it logical? It is exactly the thing they cannot compare it to. I mean, they get thrown at them a lot of syllables and the one thing that they cannot get is the relative length. How can you then be so sure that it is the relative length that is decisive. One might logically argue the other way round. There must be something else in that 4th tone which you have put in which is the thing that they do hear in spite of the fact that they get all the tones in the same duration.

I am glad to see that length is important in the 3rd tone. I was just looking at this paper of mine where I wrote on the phonological analysis of Peking (Bulletin du cercle Linguistique de Copenhague. 1966), where I tried to get out as many features as possible, but not in any experimental way. I just took what other experimentors have given us. I checked the Mandarin tone manifestations for such things as high, low, rising, falling, pitch, glottal attack, voiced attack, lengthening of main vowel, opening of main vowel, loss of main vowel, and tonality, and tried to see what came out that might be the actual distinctive features. I found that the length seemed to be important for the 3rd tone whatever else you could say about it, since it is the feature which is present in most manifestations, and I am very willing to accept your results, but I am just not sure that the results follow directly from what you have said here. One is the more eager to be sure about them for historical reasons, so I hope that a lot of checks against other possibilities will be carried out in such a way that this will also be applicable directly for comparison with other dialects, as Rygaloff said. Peking is rather characteristic with respect to what one might expect to find in Chinese dialects and Cantonese is more characteristic for what you think you might find in Thai languages.

Kratochvil: I very much agree with your suggestion to design good tones first and then start with distortions. This would, of course, be the best procedure in ideal conditions. Such conditions do not, however, exist in present-day technology. Perhaps I should describe at this point the actual conditions in which the material was synthesized. The machine I used, which was one of the computer controlled formant synthesizers of the Bell Telephone Laboratories in Murray Hill, New Jersey, one of the most advanced of its kind, was operated in the following way. You had twelve parameters to play with, i.e. you approached the sound you wished to synthesize from twelve different viewpoints, and in each case you designed the given property of the sound by taking time samples every ten msec. For example, you concentrated in turn on the fundamental frequency, the frequency of the first formant, the amplitude of the first formant, etc., and in each case you specified their values at every ten msec. of the duration of the whole sound. This was done by typing these values, according to a set of rules, on the computer's typewriter: when you typed in all the necessary values, you then asked the computer to make the actual synthesizer produce the respective sound. The computer and the synthesizer worked, of course, incredibly fast, the weak link was the typist. At best, it took about forty minutes to type in a set of four syllables with all the trimmings. And this was only the mechanical typing, one must further consider the time spent on the analysis preceding the synthesis. This means that to include in the experiment all the things you were suggesting, one would need perhaps several years during which continuous access to a speech synthesis facility would be part of the necessary conditions. This obviously was not practicable. All I could do for this experiment was to concentrate on the critical area of the borderline between full tone perception and no tone perception. The identification of that area is, of course, questionable. You could say that the area I chose was not the most critical one, or that it was too small. Whatever the case, in the present-day conditions, it is hardly possible to do more than concentrate on critical areas in experiments of this kind. We are still very far away from the feasibility of investigating all the important aspects of a phonetic issue by speech synthesis.

As to the association between pitch and tones being older than phonology, this is obviously true. However, I think that in the phonology era the word pitch began to have a different meaning than it had earlier, and this is where the confusion really rests. When one said that what made tones different from each other was pitch, and one did not define what pitch was, there was nothing wrong with the statement, however unhelpful it may have been: the word pitch was, in that case, just another word for tone. However, in the period of modern linguistics, one tends to understand by pitch or rather associate with it a precise acoustic property of sound, i.e. fundamental frequency, and one thus gets the concept that tone equals pitch equals fundamental frequency. It is this oversimplification where the problem arises from. So the approach to tone as a pitch feature is older than phonology but the really harmful oversimplification it has led to is not.

Egerod: But on the other hand even phonemicists have done more to interpret the word in this way, like Hockett, who in the clearest fashion says
that tone is not just pitch, much clearer than any non-phonemicist before
him. My point is that it is not the result of phonemic considerations. You
can go about it in a phonemic way and still forget about pitch in one or
another sense.

Kratochvil: Yes, this is true. What I was trying to suggest was that the
oversimplification is the result of the phonological state of mind rather
than of any specific phonemic considerations.

About the onset features being excluded, the only reason for this was simply
observation. In modern Peking Dialect the fundamental frequency characteristics of onset noises, i.e. anything that precedes the homogeneous column
of harmonics representing the vowel peak, are so erratic that they obviously
do not contribute to the buildup of tones.

Egerod: Is it not a case of not using informants from the same place?

Kratochvil: No. This observation is based on large-scale analysis of material from different informants and different speech conditions.

I would also like to comment on the question of 4th tone identification. How
did one come to the conclusion that it was identified according to the duration of syllables. The reason there was not so much the response to the
4th tone itself but the fact that when syllables with other tones were contracted, there was a very strong tendency to interpret these as having the
4th tone. I do not really see what other conclusions one could come to.
On the one hand, you get the phenomenon that syllables with the 4th tone,
when they become unusually short, are still interpreted as the 4th tone, and,
on the other hand, syllables with other tones are also interpreted as having
the 4th tone when they become unusually short.

Egerod: I admit it is a possible conclusion, but is it not equally possible
that there is something present in the three other tones which is not present in the 4th and this you remove, and therefore people think it is the
4th tone. It may not be duration.

Kratochvil: What could it be?

Egerod: I don't know. Say that people listen for non-falling tonality and this
becomes so obscure, that if it is not non-falling it is falling. I admit it will
cost terribly much to check it, but maybe one day the price will go down.

Egerod: I do find it very intriguing that the development of dialects which are not typical pitch tone languages does take place in those areas next to non-tonal languages. E.g. a typical tone language like Cantonese occurs where it is a close as possible to an area where they probably did speak Thai before. One does get the impression that there is some kind of fusion or bilinguism or something going on here which divides China into those two zones.

Malmqvist: I read somewhere an investigation of the tonal features of a great many compounds. It shows a preponderance for certain tonal clusters and if that is a tendency it means that the whole phonology of the Chinese language has to be changed.

In Pekingese during the last 20 years a great many changes of tone have occurred. It seems that a normalization is taking place. But who decides on the conventionalization. Is it a question of dialect influence or how does it come about?

Kratochvil: There is such a thing as language fashion which seems to be of some importance for things of this kind. There are many questions involved in this, including political considerations, so I think it would be very difficult to come to any conclusions about this in a few words. What roughly happens in China nowadays is that when variations and ambiguities penetrate into the emerging standard, a certain government committee or board set up for this purpose investigate the matter, come to a decision eliminating the ambiguity, and a directive is issued to the editorial bodies in the sphere of mass media. After the chosen variant has been heard and read exclusively for a period of time, it becomes a fashion to use it instead of the others. This is, for example, what happened to what used to be the free variants "gàosong" and "gàosu": it was decided a few years ago that "gàosu" was the correct form in the standard language, and "gàosong" has since then all but disappeared from Peking Dialect.

Göran Malmqvist

ON FORMAL CRITERIA FOR THE DETERMINATION OF THE RELATIONS OBTAINING BETWEEN CHINESE TEXTS

The present discussion is confined to two texts, the Gongyang juann and the Guuliang juann. The two texts share the following characteristics:

i.   both comment on the Chuenchiou canon;

ii.   both employ a catechetical exposition;

iii.   both utilize a strict formulaic style;

iv.   both employ functional variation of morphemes as a means of achiev-
ing economy of expression: 地   dih "to indicate the locality"; 名
ming "to name by personal name"; 氏   shyh "to name by surname";
囯   gwo "to represent as a state"; 夫人 furen "to represent as
a spouse";

v.   both employ certain morphemes in a highly specialized meaning:
致會 jih huey "to include the meeting [from which the duke of
Luu returned] in the report of his return to Luu".

Traditional comparative studies of the two texts (see William Hung's pre-
face to the Harvard-Yenching Index to the Chuenchiou and the three com-
mentaries) have been based (i) on considerations of content, and particularly on the relations of the differing praise-and-blame interpretations to
the eternal truths of Confucian dogma, (ii) on considerations of the early
transmissions of the texts, and (iii), though to a lesser extent, on considerations of parallel passages.

Different conclusions have been drawn from these earlier studies. It has
been suggested that the one text is primary and that the other is secondary

41

(A → B; B → A); that bothttexts derive from a common, written or oral, source (A ← X → B), and, finally, that the two texts were composed at about the same time and independently of one another.

An attempt will be made in this paper to establish purely formal criteria to determine whether the two texts are related, and, if so, to determine the nature of the relation obtaining between the two texts. The following types of criteria will be employed:

i.   statistical criteria;
ii.   phonological criteria;
iii. stylistic criteria;
iv.   grammatical criteria.

Statistical criteria

The Chuenchiou text comprises 1885 entries.

The Gongyang comments on 550 entries and lacks comments on 1335 entries

The Guuliang comments on 750 entries and lacks comments on 1135 entries.

The following symbols are used to indicate the concurrence, or otherwise, of the Gongyang and the Guuliang entries: ++ (both Gongyang and Guuliang comment), 00 (neither Gongyang nor Guuliang comments), +0 (only Gongyang comments), and 0+ (only Guuliang comments). The concurrences, or otherwise, of the Gongyang and Guuliang entries are shown in the following table:

	Gongyang	Guuliang
++	460/ 550 = 83.6/00	460/ 750 = 61.2/00
00	1045/1335 = 78.3/00	1045/1135 = 92.1/00
+0	90/ 550 = 16.4/00	
0+		290/ 750 = 38.8/00

The instances of ++ and 00 would seem to indicate an interdependency between the two texts compatible with one of the following relations: Gong → Guu, Guu → Gong, or Gong ← X → Guu. As to the instances of +0 and 0+ the following statistics of the average number of characters per entry may be significant. (In order to determine whether these figures are significant or not a calculation of the standard deviation of characters per entry would be required.)

<u>Gongyang</u>

characters/entry, overall average	50.19
characters/entry, in ++ instances	54.22
characters/entry, in +0 instances	29.57

<u>Guuliang</u>

characters/entry, overall average	32.37
characters/entry, in ++ instances	39.37
characters/entry, in 0+ instances	21.23

These statistics, while uncertain in the absence of a calculation of the standard deviation, are compatible with either one of the following relations between the texts: <u>Gong</u> → <u>Guu</u>, <u>Guu</u> → <u>Gong</u>, or <u>Gong</u> ← X → <u>Guu</u>.

Phonological criteria

With the exception of one rimed passage in the Gongyang (two rimes) the texts contain no rimes. Some phonological information may be gained from a comparison of the variants of proper nouns occurring in the two texts. The following tabulation accounts also for the variants obtaining in the Tzuoojuann. We find a total number of 228 variants (x, y, z) in the three texts. The distribution of these variants is as follows:

Gongyang	Guuliang	Tzuoojuann	
x	y	y	126 instances
x	x	y	49 "
x	y	x	44 "
x	y	z	9 "

A few instances of variation contain purely graphic variants (e.g. 輙/輒).

Some instances of variation may be attributed to scribes' errors (e.g.
王/壬 戊/成 于/千

In some cases the variation is of a non-phonetic nature (e.g.
天王/天子 許男/許伯 公子/公孫

In the great majority of cases the variation is clearly phonological. Some of these variations show the retention of certain archaic features, such as the presence of final voiced stop consonants (e.g. 繆 mliŏg/移 miôk; 舍 siăg/婼 t'niak; 州 tiôg/ 祝 tiôk; 弋 diək/ 姒 dzɪeg); and the presence of final -r (e.g. 陳 d'iĕn/ 夷 diər; 晉 tsiĕn/齊 dz'iər.

In some instances of variation one may be tempted to detect an influence of sandhi (e.g 祝阿 tiok - ·â / 祝柯 tiok - kâ; 醫如 ·iən - niag/ 意如 ·iəg-nia

In a small number of instances the variants reflect a base which comes closer to the phonology of Ancient Chinese than to that of Archaic Chinese (e.g. 祁黎 di - liər → źi-liei / 時來 diəg-ləg → źi-lâi

The results to be gained from a thorough investigation of these variants would seem to be compatible with the traditional notion of a long oral tradition of the texts.

Stylistic criteria

Both texts employ a strict style, involving what Hans Frankel (CYYY 39:2) terms formulas and formulaic expressions. The favourite Gongyang expressions are the following:

[此]其[不] V [x] 何	[tsyy] chyi [buh] V [x] her? (224 instances)
此其言 x 何	'Why does the CC here use the term x?'
此其稱 x 何	'Why does the CC here use the appellation X?'
其地何	'Why does the text record the place?'
其日何	'Why does the text record the day?'
其名何	'Why does the text record the personal name?'
[此]何以不 V [x]	[tsyy] her yii [buh] V [x]? (276 instances)
此何以書	'Why was this recorded here?'
此何以致	'Why was the report of the return recorded here?'
何以不言 x	'Why was the term x not used?'
何以致 x	'Why was x mentioned in the report of the return?'
x 者何	x jee her? (281 instances)

The Guuliang is less strictly patterned and frequently makes use of explanatory clauses where the Gongyang prefers the question-and-answer formulas: 不日, 其盟渝也; 于焉, 遠也; 其志, 不及事也; 不正其外交, 故弗與也; 大夫日卒, 正也; 日葬, 故也; 大夫弑其君, 以国氏者, 嫌也.

The favourite Guuliang formula is the following:

45

[此]其[不] V [x]何也   [tsyy] chyi [buh] V [x] her yee?

(143 instances)

此其不名何也   'Why does the CC not record the person-al name here?'

此其致之何也   'Why does the CC include it in the report of the return?'

其不地何也   'Why does the CC not record the place?'

The favourite Gongyang expression [tsyy] her yii [buh] V [x] is found 12 times in the Guuliang. In addition we find 12 instances of [tsyy] her yii [buh] V [x] yee.

The favourite Gongyang expression x jee her? is found 12 times in the Guuliang. In addition we find 16 instances of X jee her yee?

We find, on the one hand, that Gongyang adhers to a strict and consistent patterning and, on the other, that Guuliang while employing favourite formulas of its own at the same time uses formulas which are identical with the favourite expressions of the Gongyang. It is tempting to interpret this fact as indicating that Guuliang occasionally has allowed its style to be influenced by that of the Gongyang. It is, of course, also conceivable that the greater consistency of style of the Gongyang is the result of a strict normization of a common oral or written text.

Grammatical criteria

A perusal of the two texts leaves the reader with the impression that Gongyang adheres to a grammatical structure which reflects properties of a diachronic stage earlier than that of Guuliang. We must, however, keep in mind that what may appear as diachronically distinct grammatic-al features may perhaps equally well be explained as dialectal features operating on the same synchronic level of the language. It is worth noting, in this context, that the earliest commentary on the Gongyang, that of

Her Shiou (2nd century A.D.) in a number of cases attributes lexical items to the idiom of the Chyi area.

A great many difficulties are involved in determining diachronically different features of grammar. We may find that a number of works, A, B, and C, are dated on the basis of non-formal criteria:

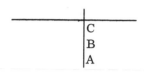

Investigators of the grammar of these works may then proceed on the assumption that the grammatical features of A are "older" than those of B, etc. Reliance on non-formal criteria may therefore obscure the picture.

We may also find that the grammatical development is obscured by the investigator's wish to establish neat and consistent diachronic paradigms. An example of this is G. Kennedy's discussion of the passive (ZH Guide).

Kennedy establishes the following paradigm:

1. A V B   <u>Wang luh chern</u>   'The king executed the minister'

2. B V iu A <u>Chern luh iu wang</u>   'The minister was executed by the king'

3. <u>B yee A suoo V yee</u>

4. <u>B yee A jy suoo V yee</u>

5. <u>B wei A suoo V</u>

The point that Kennedy makes is that <u>suoo V</u> functions as a nominal expression, 'that which was verbed upon'. The nominal function of <u>suoo V</u> is indicated by pattern 4. in which the agent of the action, A, is subordinated to the <u>suoo V</u> complex by means of the particle <u>jy</u>. The nominal status of this type of construction is further born out, says Kennedy, by the fact that the copula-verb <u>wei</u> may be used to link the two nominal expressions together, as in pattern 5.

Kennedy's paradigm is useful. We may find individual texts in which Kennedy's patterns operate. On the other hand this paradigm may to a certain extent obscure the appreciation of the historical development of the "passive" constructions in classical Chinese.

While Kennedy's first pattern appears already in early bronze inscriptions and is commonly found throughout the classical period and in such

Hann texts as the Shyyjih and the Hannshu, his 5th pattern, B wei A suoo V, is exceedingly rare in Pre-Hann texts. A few examples may be found:

Moh Tzyy: Woo wei Tian jy suoo buh yuh, Tian yih wei woo suoo buh yuh
'If I am rejected by Heaven, then Heaven is also rejected by me'

Guan Tzyy: Yeou chyr ren jee, yeou wei ren jy suoo jyh jee.
'There are those who regulate others; there are those who are regulated by others'

Tzuoojuann: Wei chyi suoo der jee guan erl chu jy.
'As to those which had been obtained by them, they put them in coffins and sent them out' (The story tells how the garrison of a besieged city, fearing that their own grave-yards would be violated by the enemy, put the bodies of the enemy soldiers who had been killed when they attempted to scale the walls, into coffins and sent them out of the city.)

It would seem that the B wei A suoo V-construction has developed out of the construction B wei A V, which is quite common in Pre-Hann texts. A few examples:

Luenyeu: Buh wei jeou kuenn   'Was not overcome by wine'
Tzuoojuann: Jyy, wei san jiun huoh   'If we stop, we shall be captured by the three armies'
Tzuoojuann: Chiee jiun charng wei Jinn jiun tsyh yii   'And, furthermore, the Lord was once given a present by the Lord of Jinn'

Wei, in these instances, would seem to function as a coverb (preposition), comparable to the modern coverbs bey, jiaw, geei, which serve to introduce the agent. (A different view is taken by Ga Ming-kae, who argues that the "passive" wei functions as a copula and that the following two sentences are structurally identical:

Chi tzyy wei luh   'His wife and children were executed'
Chi tzyy wei nu   'His wife and children were made slaves'

Wang Lih (Hannyeu shyygao) suggests that the construction B wei A suoo V did not appear until Hann time and that it must be regarded as an analogical extension of the wei-construction without suoo. He argues as follows:

"In Pre-Chyn times suoo was a pronominal form placed immediately before a transitive verb. This transitive verb was not normally followed by an object. In the construction where wei functions as a coverb, the transitive verb was likewise not followed by an object. Since the verbs in these two constructions had identical status, the suoo came to be inserted before the verb in the wei-construction. This suoo had entirely lost its pro-nominal function and become a verb-suffix." Wang Lih draws a parallel between the wei-suoo construction and the modern bey-suoo construction, common in pre-modern vernacular texts and also quite common in the writings of Mao Zedong: bey Meeigwo dih-gwo juuyih suoo chinliueh (most speakers of Mandarin would normally use the verb prefix geei in these constructions).

The interpretation of "passive" wei as a copula seems to have originated with Maa Jiann-jong, who quotes a Hannshu example: Wey taytzyy wei Jiang Chong suoo bay [jy ren] 'The Crown Prince of Wey was defeated by Jiang Chong'. This interpretation was opposed first by Yang Shuh-dar, in his emendations to the Maashyh wentong, and later by Wang Lih.

After this excursion we now return to the main topic. Gongyang frequent-ly exhibits certain idiosyncratic grammatical forms which are never, or extremely rarely, found outside the Gongyang text. A few examples:

其諸吾仲孫與

其諸以病桓與

其諸侍御有不在側者與

其諸此之謂與

其諸為其雙雙而俱至者與

其諸則宜於此焉變矣

其諸君子樂道堯舜之道與

Apart from these seven instances I have found only one other instance of this construction in the classical literature, viz. in the Luenyeu:

其諸異乎人之求之與

(This construction is obviously related to constructions such as

或諸　乎,其者乎,或者　與

which are found in Hann texts. For this see Jou Faa-gau, Substitution, pages 234 and 411.)

Another typical Gongyang expression is 走之　'to leave and go to x'

(7 instances); this may be an elliptic form for 走而之 (1 instance).

A further example is 於其 焉 'At the time of this V-ing; on the occasion of his V-ing'.

Some of these typical Gongyang expressions are occasionally found in works attributed to scholars of mid and late Hann. It is interesting to note that many instances of this Gongyang influence are found in the writings attributed to the alleged Guuliang scholar Liou Shianq, such as Shuo yuann and Shin shiuh:

Shuo yuann (Wann yeou wen kuh ed), page 131

陽虎為難於魯走之齊

Loc.cit., page 193 延陵季子適齊. 於其反也

Jenq Shyuan (Jenqshyh shypuu shiuh, apid Jingdean shyhwen):

其諸君子亦有樂於是與

A thorough comparative grammatical study of the two texts would, to my mind, involve an analysis of the following grammatical forms and processes:

Sentence suffixes
    interrogative
    non-interrogative
Sentences
    nominal predications
        copulative
        non-copulative
    non-nominal predications
        preverbal modifiers
            negatives
            other adverbials
            prepositional phrases
        postverbal modifiers
            objects
            prepositional phrases
        pivot constructions
    included predications
        subordinated clauses
            marked
            unmarked

                    included predications functioning as subject, object, etc
                          marked
                          unmarked
Coordination

                    nominal expressions
                          marked
                          unmarked
                    non-nominal expressions
                          marked
                          unmarked
Subordination

                    nominal expressions
                          marked
                          unmarked

I am as yet unable to communicate the results of this projected study.
I shall therefore, during the seminar, confine myself to some remarks
aimed at indicating the lesser degree of homogeneity of the grammatical
structure of Guuliang as compared to that of Gongyang.

While clearly indicating the dependency between the two texts the criteria
discussed here give no conclusive testimony as to the nature of the dependency. It would therefore be necessary to correlate the results of an
investigation carried out along these lines to the results gained from an
investigation based on non-formal criteria.

It appears to me that the formal analysis outlined in this paper could be
successfully applied to texts such as the Tzuoojuann and the Gwoyeu and
to texts attributed to one author, such as the Shin shiuh and the Shuo
yuann.

DISCUSSION ON MALMQVIST'S PAPER: "ON FORMAL CRITERIA FOR THE DETERMINATION OF THE RELATIONS OBTAINING BETWEEN CHINESE TEXTS".

Graham: one thing I was wondering was in connection with parallells in Gongyang and Guuliang. If there are an appreciable number of them one would suppose that comparing the parallel passages might reveal consistent features which might suggest borrowings from the one to the other.

Malmqvist: There are a number of absolute parallels. And then you have a number of cases introduced by: "juann iue","the commentary says". And in about 6 cases the "juann" could very well refer to the Gongyang juann. But then it depends on what exactly does "juann" mean. Does it mean tradition, does it mean hearsay. Hightower in his translation of the Han shih wai chuan has the notion that "juann" simply means "tradition", "tradition has it that...", "it has been transmitted that...".

Graham: What about comparisons with Tzuoojuann?

Malmqvist: Tzuoojuann comprises two parts, one part is a commentary to Chuenchiou and works obviously in the same way as Gongyang and Guuliang with "why this" and "why that". And then you have the narrative part and I think it is quite clear that the commentary part of it was added some time in early Hann. It could be interesting to compare the Tzuoojuann commentary part with the Gongyang and Guuliang and see where the correspondance are.

Graham: You mention the phonetic differences between proper names, that some of them go with archaic features and so forth. Is there any correlation between one text and the other? Is there any consistent tendency to use one sound in one text and another one in the other?

Malmqvist: No, I don't think so.

Graham: You mention the inconsistencies in Guuliang. I do not see that the inconsistencies by themselves point to an earlier date of the Gongyang.

Malmqvist: No, they don't. But when you compare the Gongyang with the

Guuliang you find that there is a strong tendency towards consistency in the Gongyang, while the Guuliang appears to borrow elements from the Gongyang. The greater consistency of the Gongyang could be a matter of later normalization. In the case of the copula you will find that Gongyang consistently uses 為 and Guuliang has 為 and three instances of 是 . The copula 是 I think is one of the forms where you really can say that the copula 是 is a development of the resumptive demonstrative pronoun 是 . The copula is a later form that does not occur in Gongyang.

Egerod: I was thinking of your example 何以知其是陳君也 No doubt it ends up with being completely identical with 其為 , but don't you think the reason is that it could also fit into that pattern before this transition takes place. It is as if it might have started out with a genitive kind of 其 "of them" or something like 其誰 "of them, who", "of these, this one", which is a possible thing to say and then that so easily gets to mean the other thing. It is the same thing with 是 where you can see how we get from the first meaning to the last meaning but we can never be sure with any specific sentence inbetween whether it is one or the other. I just question whether we can really know if 是 is a copula in this text or not. It could easily become one.

Graham: Is it really more impressive then Mencius 鈞是人也 "They are equally men"?

Egerod: Yes, one could not be sure whether these transitions have already taken place.

Graham: I would like to ask a question about this 其諸 . I have never seen the last example but one.

Malmqvist: What it means is: "could it possibly be that it would be fitting to indicate the vicissitude her". 此 in this text is always "here".

Egerod: May I ask once more about the phonological criteria. You have these wonderful examples of mljŏg, mjŏk, śjăg, t'njak, etc, what I in the Danish tradition going back to Kurt Wulff would like to look at as infixes. Are there many of those?

Malmqvist: You find about a handful with these "l" and "n" infixes.

Egerod: And "m" infixes too.

Malmqvist: Yes.

Egerod: I find it quite intriguing that this is exactly what you would expect, if these are infixes, that people would sometimes write the one with and sometimes the one without at that period when infixes seem to have lost their extra meaning, and then it would be just right that this happens. It would be very nice if there were a lot of examples. It we follow the Wulff interpretation the infix may be in the other one of your pairs, but that is another matter.

A.C. Graham

THE GRAMMAR OF THE MOHIST DIALECTICAL CHAPTERS

The six dialectical chapters of <u>Mo-tzu</u> (ch. 40, 41 經 <u>Canons</u> 42, 43 經說 <u>Explanations</u> 44 大取 <u>Ta-ch'ü</u> 45 小取 <u>Hsiao-ch'ü</u>) do not on first acquaintance affect one as likely to provide a promising field of grammatical study. Concerned with topics seldom discussed elsewhere in early Chinese literature (logic, optics, mechanics) they constitute one of the obscurest and most controversial of pre-Han documents. Indeed the present study was begun solely with the practical end of providing a further tool for interpretation. But it soon became clear that the grammatical usages of the later Mohists are of great interest in themselves. Their syntax has a lucidity and consistency which may well be unique in the history of Classical Chinese, and it shows up the logical structure of the language with unequalled clarity.[1]

Pre-Han literature reflects the historical stages and the diverging local dialects of a rapidly developing language, so that nearly every text is to some extent peculiar in grammar as well as in vocabulary. Inside the Mohist corpus, which accumulated over a long period (c. 400-200 BC), we can discern pronounced general differences between the ancient core (<u>Mo-tzu</u> ch. 8-37) and the dialectical and military chapters, and less obvious differences even inside the groups of cognate chapters. In the dialectical chapters, as we shall see, the grammar of the Ta-ch'ü and Hsiao-ch'ü is not quite the same as that of the Canons and Explanations. We need to know as much as possible about the grammar of these writings since we can be sure that an ordinary knowledge of Archaic Chinese usage, however wide the reading experience on which it is based, will often be inadequate and even treacherous when applied to texts dealing with such unfamiliar subjects as logic, optics and mechanics. Obscure Chinese texts tempt us to force meaning out of the apparently meaningless on the assumption that their grammar is exceptionally loose. But this is a short-sighted indulgence; only if their grammar turns out to be strict can we hope to read them with any confidence.

The later Mohists, more than any other Chinese philosophical school, were concerned with logical precision, to which grammatical precision is an essential means. We should therefore expect in principle a grammar of exceptional strictness, the study of which might be relevant to the whole question of the possibilities and limitations of the Chinese language as an instrument of analytic thought. But this general consideration hardly prepares us for the precision and consistency of the grammatical system as we actually find it. We may note in the first place the almost complete absence of rhetorical usages. For example there are no exclamatory sentence patterns; the exclamatory final particle tsai 哉 is absent, the final hu 乎 is purely interrogative, we find ch'i 其 as the possessive pronoun ("his, her, its, their") but not as a pre-verbal modal particle. Indeed there are no final particles at all except for yeh

也 , hu, yü 與 (= yeh hu 也乎) and occasionally the perfective

yi 矣 . The only rhetorical questions are a couple in the Hsiao-ch'ü

(我奚獨不.... "Why shouldn't I too....", 吾豈.... "How

can I.....?"); otherwise all questions expect answers. The manner in

which particles serve only the logical structure of the sentence can be

seen in the use of the pre-verbal particles yi 亦 yu 又 "also, again".

which in many pre-Han texts contribute to idiomatic constructions which

are very difficult to analyse. In the dialectical chapters their functions

stand out nakedly and are sharply differentiated, with yi referring back-

ward, generally to the subject, and yu (always written with the graph 有)

referring forward to the verb or object:

B 23 　所鑒大，景亦大．

"What is mirrored is big, and the shadow too is big."

B 33 　知是之非此也，有知此之不在此也．

"Knowing that the one in question is not this, knowing too that it is not

here......."

The Canons and Explanations are perhaps unique among pre-Han texts in

having no pronouns or particles which are logical synonyms:

yü	與	"together with"	Not chi	及
yü	與	(= yeh hu)	Not yeh	邪
tz'ǔ	此	"this"	Not ssǔ	斯
tzǔ	自	"from"	Not yu	由

ho	何	"what"	Not hsi	奚	ho	曷
wu	惡	"to, in, from what?"	Not an	安	yen	焉
yi	已	"already"	Not chi	既		
ch'ieh	且	"about to"	Not chiang	將		
yu	猶	"still"	Not shang	尚		
fang	方	"just now"	Not shih	適		
tse	則	"(if......) then"	Not ssŭ	斯	chi	即
ku	故	"therefore	Not shih-yi	是从		
erh hou	而後	"only then"	Not jan hou	然後		
jo	若	"if, like"	Not ju	如		
chü	俱	"all" (external distributive, pre-verbal)	Not chieh	皆		
chin	盡	"all" (internal distributive)	Not hsi	悉		

The handful of apparent exceptions are in passages commonly agreed to be corrupt (A 12 將　B 25 如　), or use the word in another sense (適　"merely"), or allow an alternative interpretation which the uniformity of usage entitles us to prefer (A 11 使人(如)知己 "enable others to know one"; A 46, an Illustration misplaced to A 48, 若斯 "For example, cutting off"; A 99 皆(=偕)入　"enter together"). We find some innovations in the Ta-ch'ü and Hsiao-ch'ü (chi for yi "already", kou 尚 "if" as well as jo and jan hou as well as erh hou); whether these imply a new tolerance of synonyms or a further refining of distinctions will be considered in due course (p. 106-108)

There is some reason to suppose that besides avoiding synonyms the Mohists graphically distinguished pronouns and particles commonly written with the same character. Evidence of this survives in the case of chih 之 as pronoun and as particle. [2] It is remarkable also that in the present text yü "together with", yü (yeh hu) and chü "lift"[3] are all written with the graph 與 , yet chü "mention, pick out an object by a name" is distinguished from chü "lift" by the radical (擧) while yü 與 "give to" is avoided in favour of yü 予 . Such distinctions hardly make sense unless there were further distinctions obliterated by graphic standardisation. That level-tone and rising-tone yü were somehow distinguished is suggested by such an apparently clumsy sentence as the following, which we deliberately leave unpunctuated (the phrases in inverted commas are quoted from the Canon):

B 2   獸與生鳥與「物盡」與「大小」也

(Explanation) " 'Is it an animal?' and 'Is it a living thing? Is it a bird?', are 'the things all included' and 'a bigger or a smaller' "

Sentence structure

Writers in Western languages who find themselves in the position of having to quote from these imperfectly understood documents seem often to be translating on the assumption that they are dealing with fragmentary

59

notes rather than consecutive sentences. It may therefore be advisable to state plainly from the start that the later Mohists wrote true sentences, not less but more strictly organised than those of other pre-Han writers. The <u>Canons</u> of one series in Part A (A 76-87) simply list meanings of a word (A 76 「已」.成.亡 "'Finish': make complete, abolish"), and a few in Part B are nominalised clauses exposed in front of the summing-up formula (B 77 學之益也說在誹者 "That learning is useful: the explanation is in the objector"); with these exceptions sentences can always be identified when the text is intelligible at all. Even headings in the <u>Explanations</u> are tied to the succeeding sentences; when nominal they are treated as subject (B 4 「一二」不相盈 "'One and two' do not fill each other") or as exposed element resumed by a pronoun (A 1 「小故」,有之不必然 "In the case of the 'minor cause', when we have it this will not necessarily be so", cf also B 25, 39), when verbal they behave as preliminary clauses (B 26 「挈」,長重者下 "When you 'pull up', the longer and heavier is below", cf also B 11).

As in Classical Chinese generally, it is convenient to distinguish between the verbal sentence (with a main verb precedable by <u>pu</u> 不 "not") and the nominal sentence (with a complement precedable by <u>fei</u> 非 "is not"), although we shall see shortly that the nominal sentence presents certain complications:

Verbal sentence

Subject	Verb	Object (substitutable by chih 之)	Directive (preceded by yü 於 , substitutable by yen 焉)
B 18 (二)光	夾	(一)光	

"Two lights flank one light"

| B 19 | 成 | 景 | 於 上 |

"It forms a shadow above"

| B21 景 | 大 | | 於 水 |

"The shadow is bigger than the piece of wood"

Hsiao-ch'ü NO 16 馬 　 (或)白

"Some horse is white"

Nominal sentence

Subject	Negative	Complement (followed by yeh 也)

Hsiao-ch'ü NO 13

(白)馬 　　　　 馬 也

"A white horse is a horse"

| B 67 | 非 | 牛 也 |

"It is not an ox".

Subordinate units (such as those bracketed) precede a sentence position.

The subject itself, although for present purposes it is convenient to treat it as a sentence position, can be seen as a unit subordinate to the sentence pattern as a whole.

The later Mohists are notable for the rigour with which they adhere to the standard word-order of the verbal sentence. With certain exceptions which will be considered later (p. 128-129) the directive is never exposed at the head of the sentence, and instrumental phrases with yi 以 , however lengthy, precede the verb as subordinate units. We find none of the inverted patterns common in other texts except for four cases in the Ta-ch'ü(EC 7-10) of "X 之謂 Y", "It is X that is called Y", serving to contrast the "X" units of four successive definitions. Exposure is governed by a firm rule: the exposed unit (or its subject if it is a nominalised clause) is in apposition with a resumptive pronoun inside the sentence structure:

1. Apposition with object chih

B 57 楹之搏也，見之 ....

"In the case of the pillar being round, when you see it....."

(cf. also A 1, B 48, Ta-ch'ü NO 1)

In negative sentences chih is omitted and the ordinary negatives replaced by fu   and wu   (for the extreme consistency of this cf. p. 77, 78):

A 83 *可者，用而勿必

"The admissible, employ but do not treat as certain...."

(followed by two more examples)

B 27 凡重，上弗挈．．．．

"All weight, if you do not pull it up from above . . . ."

(followed by two more examples, cf. also B 39).

We may also note a case of two exposed units resumed by adverbial

"huo . . . . . huo . . . . .":

B 53 〈?〉, 霍, 或 以 名 視 (=示) 人, 或 以 實 視 人

"With (?) and with soup, in one case we show to others by means of the

name and in one case by means of the object."

2. Apposition with directive yen:

B 25 衡 木, *加 重 焉 . . . .

"The cross-bar, if you put a weight on it . . ."

3. Apposition with the "X" of the "X chih" substitutable for ch'i:

B 25 衡, 加 重 於 其 一 旁 . . . .

"The steelyard, if you put a weight on one side of it . . . ."

(cf. also A 64, B 39, 57, 74).

4. Apposition with complement shih or mou:

Ta-ch'u NO 2 諸 以 形 貌 命 者, 若 山 丘 室 廟 者
皆 是 也

"As for those which name according to shape and features, such ones

as 'mountain', 'mound', 'house' and 'shrine' are all examples of

these."

以形貌命者，必智是之某也，焉智某也

"As for those which name according to shape and features, it is necessary to know that this is "X", only in it does one know X."

5. Apposition with two subjects, the first qualified by shih:

B 53 堯之義也，是聲也〈生〉於今，所義之
實處於古．

"As for Yao being an example, this vocal sound is born in the present,
the object taken as example resides in the past."

In the absence of a resumptive pronoun, even a long nominalised clause
ending in yeh is not an exposed element; its subject is the subject of the
whole sentence. In the following example the subject is chih 智 (generally written 知), "the intelligence", a concept preferred by the
Mohists to the hsin 心 "mind" of other schools:

A 75 若智之慎*之也無遺於其害也....

"If the intelligence in its consideration of it overlooks none of the harm
in it......"

Leaving aside occasional syntactically obscure passages in which one is
tempted to postulate exposure, the only type of unit which is exposed
without resumption is the single word followed by yeh che 也者
which stands at the head of the sentence eleven times in the Explanations.
This is always a word quoted from the corresponding Canon, followed by
an explanatory sentence with which it has only a loose relationship of

topic and comment, as is especially clear in the four examples in A 3-6 (cf. p. 101, 102). In one case it actually allows a second exposed element, this one attached to the sentence structure by a resumptive ch'i:

A 64 「虛」也者, 兩木之間, 謂其無木者也

"'Empty': of the interval between two pieces of wood, it refers to that of it in which there is no wood." (The interval between two pieces may be partially or wholly filled by another piece.)

"X is Y"

The later Mohists as logicians are much interested in propositions of the form "X is Y". For these they use the ordinary nominal sentence negated by fei, and are punctilious in supplying the final yeh even in the negative. But they also have occasion to negate fei itself. To do this they have to treat it as an ordinary verb, negate by pu and drop the final yeh. They also have two other verbal copulae negated by pu and used without yeh, wei 為 "constitutes, counts as, is deemed" and wei 惟 "is and only is". The sentence with copula thus resembles a verbal sentence, but with the decisive difference that the pronoun chih 之 which substitutes for the object cannot substitute for the complement:

	subject	copula	complement
B 67	牛	(不)非	牛

"The ox is not not an ox"

65

	subject	copula	complement
B 2		(俱) 為	麔
"Both count as milu deer"			
B 3		(不) 為	夫
"He is not being deemed a husband"			
B 12		惟	是
"It is this and only this"			
B 72		(不) 惟	(其) 謂
"It is not what it is called and nothing else".			

In philosophical as in other Chinese "wei 為 Y" is not quite equivalent to "Y yeh". Much as wei ch'en 為臣 is to fill the role, perform the functions, of a minister, so wei ai jen 為愛人 is to satisfy the conditions for being deemed love of mankind:

Hsiao-ch'ü NO 16 「愛人」待周愛人，而後為愛人

"'Love of man' requires that one loves men without exception, only then is it deemed to be love of man."

This use of wei is also frequent in the White Horse and Meanings and Things essays of Kung-sun Lung:

馬未與白為馬，白未與馬為白

"A horse not yet combined with white is deemed a horse, white not yet combined with horse is deemed to be white."

天下無指者，生於物之各有名，不為指也

"That meanings do not exist in the world is because each thing has a name
and is not deemed to be a meaning."

Kung-sun Lung actually appears to contrast pu wei chih "is not deemed
to be a meaning" with fei chih; his point, on my interpretation of this obscure essay,[4] is that an ox or horse has its own name and is not called
a "meaning", is not a meaning but an ox or a horse, yet we debate whether
a thing "may be said to be the meaning" (可謂指) of a name or "is
not the meaning" (非指).

The Mohists as logicians must often discuss what X is or is not without
specifying what it is or is not. But they cannot combine fei or wei with
the relative pronoun so or object chih without rendering them transitive
("what he condemns/does" "he condemns/does it"). Consequently they
use both verbs freely without complements, producing sentences in which
at first sight wei seems unintelligible and fei can be mistaken for fei
"wrong":

A 73　　或謂之牛,或謂之非牛

B 35　　或謂之是,或謂之非

"One calls it 'ox', the other calls it 'not ox'..... One calls it 'this',
the other calls it 'not this'."

Hsiao-ch'ü NO 17　人之鬼非人也,兄之鬼兄也.
　.... 此乃一是而一非者也.

"The ghost of a man is not a man, the ghost of your elder brother is your elder brother...... These are examples in which it is this in one case and is not in the other."

Ta-ch'ü NO 6 有非之異，有不然之異

"There is the difference of not being this and the difference of not being so."

B 8 假必非也而後假

"The loan-named could not be loan-named unless it were <u>not</u> this."

(<u>Fei</u> without a complement also A 73, 98, 99, <u>Ta-ch'ü</u> NO 2

<u>Hsiao-ch'ü</u> NO 5)

<u>Wei</u> is four times without a complement:

A 83 臧之為   "Jack being deemed this"

A 89 霍為   "A crane is deemed this"

<u>Hsiao-ch'ü</u> NO 5 效者為之法也，所效者，所以 為之法也.

"A copy is a standard for being deemed this. What it copies is the standard by which it is deemed this."

Both <u>fei</u> and <u>wei</u> may be preceded by <u>hsiang</u> "mutually":

A 66 異處不相盈，相非是相外也

"Different places do not fill each other. Not being each other is excluding

each other" (unique example).

B 30 刀糴相為賈

"Coin and grain are each the price of the other."

Wei 惟 is the pre-classical affirmative copula corresponding to the negative copula fei.[5] Its functions were taken over by the "X Y yeh" pattern, but it survived before the subject ("It is X which....." narrowing to "It is only X which....") and the verb ("It is that....." narrowing to "It is only that...."), as well as in front of a complement ("is only"). Historically it is difficult to determine the point at which it had ceased to function as copula and had become a particle dependent on subject and verb ("only"). In the sparse examples in the dialectical chapters (where the graphs 惟, 唯 generally represent sui 雖 "although") it appears to be a copula, since clauses containing it do not have either a final yeh or a main verb (B 11 惟所利 "It is only a matter of convenience", B 12 惟是 "It is the said thing and nothing else", B 72 惟吾謂 "It is and only is what I call it"), unless we except a case where yi might be the main verb (B 46 惟以五路 "If it is only by means of the five senses ...."). Syntactically it behaves quite differently from tu 獨 "only", which is limited to sentences with a main verb or yeh (cf. B 21 非獨小 (大) 也 "It is not only the size", B 38 必獨指吾所舉 "Be sure to point only at what I mentioned"). Wei is significant in philosophical argument only in B 12 and 72 (which has three more examples, discussed p. 96, 103); in both Sun Yi-jang took it as the expression of assent 唯 wei "Yes" used verbally ("respond"). But the argument of B 72 seems to me to make sense only on the present interpretation, in spite of one awkward sentence where I take it to be the word itself quoted from the Canon

(103). The Mohists use chih 止 "stop" to deal with a name

which "stops" in, is confined to, one thing (A 78, B 68); wei would be

suitable for dealing with a thing confined to one name.

The Ta-ch'ü sometimes contrasts an affirmative with a preceding negative

"X Y yeh" sentence by adding nai 乃 before the complement in answer

to the fei of the preceding sentence (EC 2, NO 3, cf. the corrupt EC 5).

It also uses nai to carry an equation one step further, "X Y yeh, nai Z yeh",

"X is Y, which is Z" (EC 2). Nai was also useful for pinning down an

isolated shih as complement, 乃是 "is the said thing"; we find

examples in both the Ta-ch'ü (No 4) and the Hsiao-ch'ü (No 13).

Throughout the Explanations, when verbal phrases are linked by yeh,

we frequently find the pronoun shih 是 "the said, the aforesaid" mark-

int the start of the complement. But it is not used between nominal units

in the "X Y yeh" sentence; it is a resumptive pronoun clarifying the or-

ganisation, sometimes of short linked phrases, sometimes of long se-

quences of clauses.

Pronouns

The 1st person pronouns are wu 吾 and wo 我 (the former once

subject in the Hsiao-ch'ü but otherwise possessive); in place of the 2nd

person tzŭ 子 is used; in the 3rd ch'i 其 is exclusively possessive, chih 之 object and yen 焉 directive (equivalent to yü chih 於之). There are examples of chu 諸 as a fusion of chih yü 之於 (B 16, Hsiao-ch'ü NO 10) but not of chih hu 之乎 .

Of greater linguistic interest are the demonstratives. The near demonstratives tz'ǔ 此 "this" (the thing here) and shih "this" (the said thing) are only vaguely differentiated in most pre-Han writing, but in the Canons and Explanations (although not in the Ta-ch'ü and Hsiao-ch'ü) the distinction is unexpectedly sharp. Of crucial importance in the use of shih is the fact that disputation is concerned with alternatives which are shih and fei 非 , and that these are not, as generally elsewhere, simply the "right" and the "wrong". Disputation is conceived primarily as debate as to whether a particular object is "the said thing" (shih, typically an ox. Cf. A 73, 74) or "is not" (fei). The subject of debate may of course be a general concept, and if it is particular what it is judged to be may also be singular ("North" or "South"). But in contexts of disputation shih will refer not to an object but to what is meant by a name, in the case of class names not to an ox or horse but to oxen or horses in general. Chih shih 知是 (A 94, B 38) "to know the said thing" is to know what "X" is, be able to recognise it when one sees it. In B 38 it is contrasted with chih chih 知之 "to know about them", referring to particular objects (cf. also B 41; there is, however, no restriction of chih chih to the particular in ordinary contexts). In B 1, 2, where the

71

Canons are about lei 類 "kinds of thing". the Explanations use shih

of the kind which a debater rightly or wrongly selects in arguing from

particular instances. Here there is an explicit contrast of shih and tz'ǔ:

the point of the distinction may be brought out by translating shih as "what

it is judged to be":

B 1 彼 以 此 其 然 也 説 是 其 然 也

"He, because of its being so of the thing here, explains that it is so of the

thing it is judged to be."

B 2 此 然 是 必 然 , 則 俱 為 麐

"If what is so of the thing here is necessarily so of the thing it is judged

to be, both will be the 'milu deer'."

Cf. B 33 知 是 之 非 此 也 , 有 (=又) 知 是 之 不 在 此 也 , 然 而 謂 此 「南 北」

(Of North and South, which change positions as we move) "Knowing that

what this place is judged to be is not this place, knowing too that it is not

in this place, we none the less call this place 'the North' or 'the South'."

In the Ta-ch'ü the distinction between shih and tz'ǔ has faded, no doubt

because the specialised shih has been replaced by a more satisfactory

technical term, mou 某 "X":

No 2〈諸〉以 形 貌 命 者 , 必 智 是 之 某 也 , 焉 智 某 也.

"With things named according to shape and features one must know that

this is "X", only in it does one know X."

Although in ordinary pre-Han discourse shih/fei and also jan "so" are used freely to judge propositions as right or wrong we do not find these usages in the dialectical chapters. A thing is the "said thing" (shih) and something is "so" of it (jan); a proposition is logically allowable (k'o 可) and fits the fact (tang 畺). However, we are once told explicitly that shih/fei can be said of "discourse, conduct, learning or an object" (A 89 論, 行, 學, 實, 是 非 也), and they are used of right or wrong courses of action in one Explanation and several times in the Ta-ch'ü. In spite of a couple of cases of pu shih 不 是 for fei (B 82, Hsiao-ch'ü No 13) the words when final are followed by yeh, implying that they are nominalised: "the right/wrong thing to do". Most examples are in a pattern "verb-object-wei 為 shih/fei yeh", in which shih/fei yeh seems to be an embedded "(X) Y yeh" of a kind discussed elsewhere (p. 131-133).

B 78 雖 多 誹, 其 誹 是 也

"Although he criticises a lot his criticising is the right thing to do."

EC 1 語 天 之 (=志) 為 (是 也)… 以 人 非 為 (是 也)

"Expound Heaven's will as being the right thing to do...... suppose that what others condemn is the right thing to do."

EC 8 權 非 為 (是 也), (非 非 為 非 也)

"Re-estimate the wrong as being the right thing to do, or condemn the wrong as being the wrong thing to do......"

In the case of pairs of contrasted concepts, shih marks the one under discussion:

A 26, 27 得是而喜，則是利也，其害也非是也．

得是而惡，則是害也，其利也非是也．

"If you are pleased to get this one, it is this one which is beneficial; the one of them which is harmful is not this one.

If you dislike getting this one, it is this one which is harmful; the one of them which is beneficial is not this one."

From this example we may note that ch'i "their, of them" often refers to the implied alternatives:

B 35 或　　　　"the one"/ 其或　　"the other of them"

A 46 其存者　　　　　　　　　　"the one of them which remains"

B 52 均其絕也莫絕　　　　"If we equalise the one which snaps none will snap."

With one near demonstrative a distinction is made between the independent pronoun and the pronoun as adjunct. Tz'ǔ is always the independent pronoun: A 97 取此擇彼　　"choose this, reject that": B 76 愛利此也，所愛所利彼也　"The loving and the benefiting are here, the loved and the benefited are there." The corresponding pronoun used as adjunct is chih 之 : A 39 之一　"this one", B 71 之人 "this man", Hsiao-ch'ü NO 17 之馬 "this horse", 之牛 "this ox". Shih is both independent and adjunct.

The far demonstrative pi 彼　is not simply the opposite of tz'ǔ "the one here". It is used freely in contrast with tz'ǔ and the corresponding adjunct chih but also with shih "the one in question" and wo "I":

74

A 97 取此擇彼

"Choose the one here, reject the one there"

A 31 以*之名舉彼實

"Refer to the object there by means of the name here"

A 16 為是之寡彼也，弗為也

"Because of this one interfering with the other he will not do it."

D 1 彼以此其然也說是其然也．
我以此其不然也疑是其然也．

"He, because it is so of the one here, argues that it is so of the thing it

is judged to be. I, because it is not so of the one here, doubt that it is so

of the thing it is judged to be."

In all these cases pi refers to the contrasted member of a pair of alter-

natives. When the contrast is with something indefinite the word used is

t'o 也 (=他) "other":

B 3 謂是則是固美也，謂也則是非美．

"If it refers to this one, it really is that this one is beautiful; if it refers

to another thing, it is not that this one is beautiful."

Hsiao-ch'ü No 14,15 無也故焉

"There is no other reason that this."

When a demonstrative is the subject of a nominalised phrase it is often followed by chih 之 , in accordance with the ordinary rule that the subject of a nominalised phrase is either followed by chih or is the possessive pronoun ch'i. When this is found in parallel phrases the contrast is between verbs or complements:

B 33 知是之非此也,有(=又)知是之不在此也

"Knowing that what this place is judged to be is not this place, knowing too that it is not in this place...."

B 80 是之是也非是也者 .....

"In the case of this being this or not being this......"

But we also find a demonstrative followed by ch'i. When there are parallel phrases it is the subjects which are contrasted:

B 1 彼以此其然也説是其然也

"He, because it is so of the one here, argues that it is so of the thing it is judged to be."

B 70 在室者之色若是其色

"The colour of the thing inside the house is like the colour of this."

Cf. also Ta-ch'ü EC 3 非彼其行益也

"It is not that the performance of that one is increased."

The resumptive ch'i emphasises the preceding noun in the same way that shih 是 and chih 之 emphasise the inverted object, in a familiar construction not found in the dialectical chapters (Tso chuan 宣 12/3 惟敵是求 "It is only the enemy that we seek."

There remains one more demonstrative, the adjunct fu 夫 . This is used to introduce a general concept: B 70 夫名 "Names", B 72 夫霍 "the crane", Hsiao-ch'ü NO 10 夫辯者 "disputation NO 15 夫讀書 "to read a book". In each case the context shows that the reference is to names, cranes, disputation is general, not to particular instances. There is also one example of the construction jo-fu 若夫 X, "In the case of X on the other hand....." (B 27).

Negatives

The negative verbs and particles are those general throughout pre-Han literature, and are very clearly differentiated.

1. pu 不 and 2. fu 弗 , pre-verbal negatives. The rule-of-thumb that a verb negated by fu may be translated as though it had an object chih 之 applies without exception to the fourteen examples of fu. While this is generally true of pre-Han texts of the classical period the dialectical chapters are very unusual in not only confining fu to this type of construction but also excluding pu from it, except when there is an intervening adverb. In the two cases where an adverb intervenes the negative is pu:

A 4 　不必得之 　　　"not necessarily find it"
B 38 　不能獨指 　　　"unable to point at it alone"

It may be noticed that in both cases the reference of the verb is specified, by chih "it" or by tu "alone". In the absence of an adverb the reference of

an objectless transitive verb is indefinite after pu, definite after fu:

A 13 不必得   "not necessarily succeed"

B 16 不能治   "not able to govern"

B 39 弗能指   "not able to point it out"

B 44 弗治   "not govern it"

<u>Ta-ch'ü</u> EC 2 弗能去   "not able to get rid of it"

There is none of the stylistic reluctance to repeat <u>fu</u> in parallel sentences

so common in pre-Han literature:

B 27 上弗挈，下弗收，旁弗劫....

"If you do not pull it up from above or gather it in from below or inter-

fere with it from the side....."

3. <u>wu</u> 毋   and 4. <u>wu</u> 勿   , negative imperatives. The four

examples are sufficient to confirm that, as in the other pre-Han literature

of the classical period, the relation is the same as between <u>pu</u> and <u>fu</u>:

A 83 勿必 .... 勿疑 ....勿偏

"Do not treat it as certain.....do not doubt it......do not present one of

them without the other."

B 37 毋舉吾所不舉

"Do not mention what I did not mention."

5. <u>fou</u> 否，不 , negative verb equivalent to the immediately preceding

verbal unit negated by <u>pu</u> (B 12 或復（或）否   "in one case re-

peated, in the other not", B 34 知之否 "know it or not", B 73
盈否...盈之否 "fill or not..... fill it or not", B 78 可否
"admissible or not"). In other texts it frequently stands alone in dialogue
to express denial, and this seems to be its function in one of the two cases
where in the present text it is written without the radical (A 94 諾不
"Yes or no", cf. B 52 絕不 "snap or not").

6. wei 未 "not yet". This twice follows a verb in the manner of fou
(A 89 成未 "complete or not yet complete", B 3 偏去未
"one or other rejected or not yet rejected"), a rare usage for which Chou
Fa-kao (vol. 3, p. 251n) notes only a single example (Shih chi, ch. 107,
2844/3 已盡未 "Is it already finished or not?"). We may note
the distinction between pu k'o chih 不可知 "unknowable" (B 10) and
wei k'o chih "not yet knowable" (A 75, 94, B 58, 73: opposite of hsien
chih 先知 "know beforehand", A 94, B 57), which is observed
throughout Mo-tzu. Wei k'o 未可 "not yet admissible" appears only
in B 67; there it refers to positions not yet conceded in the course of the
argument and the conclusion is marked by pu k'o "inadmissible".

7. mo 莫 "none". This has been treated with the distributives (84).

8. wu 無 "there is not, have not", opposite of yu 有 "there is,
have". We have elsewhere considered its use in front of verbs and the
reason why it is sometimes written with the graph 毋 (p. 88-98).

There are no less than four cases of pu yu 不有 (A 65, 83, 87, B 44), as well as one of wu yu "not have any" (B 66). I have failed to discover a single factor accounting for the use of pu yu instead of wu.

9. fei 非 , negative copula "is not", negating the "X Y yeh" pattern. The constant concern of the dialecticians with proving that X is or is not Y drives them to some astonishing permutations, negating fei itself by pu, preceding it by hsiang 相 "mutually", or by quantifying yu and wu, freely omitting the complement (p. 65-68).

The copula fei as main verb, whether or not it has a complement, regularly takes a final yeh; this is especially apparent in the many examples of affirmative and negative "X Y yeh" sentences throughout the Ta-ch'ü and Hsiao-ch'ü. The final yeh is missing only in the pattern "... yeh, fei...." (B 3 是固美也...是非美 "It is of course that this one is beautiful. ....It is not that this one is beautiful". Cf. also A 18, B 47). The absence of yeh may therefore be significant, as in B 60 毋與非半 "There is nothing which when combined with it is not half", which cannot be taken as "What has nothing combined with it is not half".

At several places we find the phrases 非牛,非馬 , which seem at first sight to be clauses ("it is not an ox", "It is not a horse"). But if so we should expect the yeh, which is used freely even in front of conjunctions:

B 8　假必非也而後假

"The loan-named necessarily is not the thing in question, otherwise it

would not be loan-named."

B 72　「惟吾謂」，非名也則不可

"'It is and only is what I call it' is inadmissible if it is not its name."

The phrases are in fact nominalised, "what is not an ox/horse", "a non-

ox/non-horse":

A 73　「凡牛」「區非牛」，兩也

"'All oxen' and 'non-oxen as a group' is presenting as a pair."

B 12　當「牛」「馬」．．．．．　　　"Fit 'ox' or 'horse'．．．．．．．"

A 50　當「馬」「非馬」　　　"Fit 'horse' or 'non-horse'"

We have elsewhere noticed fei niu "non-ox" in constructions which re-

quire it to be a nominal unit, after wei chih 謂之 "call it" and huo

或　　"some" (p. 86,115). The latter is found in the curious ar-

gument as to whether an ox and a horse are oxen:

B 67　或非牛而非牛也可，則或非牛或牛
而牛也可．．．．．牛不非牛，馬不非馬，
而牛馬非牛非馬無難 而牛馬

"If it is admissible that with one as a non-ox they are not oxen, it is ad-

missible that with one a non-ox and one an ox they are oxen. .... Without

the ox not being the ox or the horse not being the horse, there is no dif-

ficulty about the ox and the horse being a non-ox and a non-horse."

In the first sentence there is a clear contrast between on the one hand niu ("ox") and fei niu ("non-ox"), on the other niu yeh ("is an ox") and fei niu yeh ("is not an ox"). In the last sentence it will be seen that the absence of yeh is crucial; if it were present we should have the statement "An ox and a horse are not oxen and are not horses", which whatever it might mean does not fit the argument.

The absence of the yeh also serves to distinguish the fei of the pattern "fei.....pu/fu/wu.......", "If it is not......then not......":

Ta-ch'ü NO 10 今人非道無所行

"Now men have nowhere to walk except the Way."

This is the only construction in which the difference between fei and wu is allowed to fade:

A 83   非彼必不有

"There cannot be one without the other."

In the dialectical chapters we do not find any similar construction with wu in the place of fei, and indeed wu at the head of a sentence is the main verb and predominant over a later negative (B 36 無不讓   "There is nothing he does not yield:, B 60 毋與非半   "There is nothing which combined with it is not half").

Since the curious permutations of fei "is not" often tempt one to confuse it with fei "wrong", we list all the few examples of the latter:

A 17   作非也   "is to be wrong in taking the initiative"(?)

B 3   為非   "constitute the wrong thing to do"

Ta-ch'ü EC 1

歌天之(=志)為
非也

"sing (?) of Heaven's will as being the wrong thing to do"

EC 8 權非為是也

"re-weigh the wrong as being the right thing to do"

非非為非也

"condemn the wrong as being the wrong thing to do"

It would appear that in this usage <u>fei</u> is nominalised, "the wrong thing to do" (opposite of <u>shih</u> "the right thing to do") and that it refers exclusively to actions, not to propositions. For the construction of the three <u>Ta-ch'ü</u> examples, cf. (p. 131-133).

<u>Fei</u> "wrong" is also used causatively ("reject, condemn"), of persons as well as actions:

B 78   可 非   "rejectable"

B 79   弗 非   "does not reject it"

       非 誹   "reject criticising"

<u>Ta-ch'ü</u> EC 1   人 非   "others' condemnation" (an idiom, cf. M.344/410)

EC 8   非 非   "reject the wrong"

<u>Hsiao-ch'ü</u> NO 14, 15   自 非   "condemn oneself"

       非 之   "condemn them"

Distribution

The dialectical chapters show a theoretical interest in quantification, partly inspired by the Mohist doctrine of loving not some but all men. They define "all" as "none not" (A 43 「盡」莫不然也) and "some" as "not all" (Hsiao-ch'ü NO 5 「或」也者,不盡也), and have several quantifiers of their own, used adverbially like the regular distributive particles: chou 周 "in all cases", liang 兩 "in both cases", p'ien 偏 "in one case but not the other". It is therefore of some interest to see how they deal with the standard distributive words of Classical Chinese. These are either verbs or pre-verbal particles (some of which are basically verbs used adverbially), although in the case of universal quantification the Mohists are able to detach a noun from its context with the aid of the adjunct fan (A 73 凡牛 "all oxen"). The basic distinction is between external and internal distribution, the former relating things to each other (chü 俱 "all", as a verb "associate"), the latter relating parts or individuals within one thing or kind of thing (chin 盡 "all", as a verb "exhaust, use up"):

	External		Internal	
All	chü 俱	(verbal sentences, 28 times)	chin 盡	
	chieh 皆	(nominal sentences, 4 times)		
Some	huo 或		yu 有	
None	mo 莫		wu 無	

84

The four cases of chieh "all" are all in the Ta-ch'ü (the graph also appears in A 99, but probably for chieh 偕 "together"), while chü occurs once in the Hsiao-ch'ü but 27 times in the Canons and Explanations These figures might be interpreted to mean that the earlier documents use chü and the later chieh. But since chü is confined to verbal sentences throughout the concordanced pre-Han literature it seems safe to discount this fact as an accidental consequence of the growing prominence of the "X Y yeh" sentence after the Mohist shift of interest from the name to the sentence. It would appear that they deliberately confined chieh to nominal as well as chü to verbal sentences.

Distribution is comparatively rare in nominal sentences. We find only chieh and huo, used when there is more than one subject, and a single case of chin, referring to the parts:

Ta-ch'ü No 2 諸以形貌命者，若「山」「丘」「室」「廟」者皆是也

"As for those which name according to shape and features, such ones as 'mountain', 'mound', 'house' and 'shrine' are all examples of these."

諸非以舉量數命者，敗之盡是也

"As for those which do not name be referring to measure or number, when you break the thing up all of it is this."

In both cases with huo there is no final yeh and the whole phrase depends on a main clause elsewhere; one remains in doubt whether it was legitimate to say "huo X yeh", "One is an X":

B 65 俱有法而異，或木或石.

"All have the standard but they are different, some wood and some stone."

B 67 或非牛而牛也可，則或非牛或牛
而牛也可.

"If it is admissible that with one a non-ox they are not oxen, it is admissible that with one a non-ox and one an ox they are oxen."

We find no sentences of the form basic to Western logic, "All/some/no Xs are Ys". The Mohists write not "All white horses are horses". but simply "White horses are horses" (Hsiao-ch'ü No 13 白馬馬也), not "Some horses are white horses" but the verbal sentence "Some horse is white" (Hsiao-ch'ü No 17 馬或白). Had they been interested in sentences of this type they would presumably have used the internal distributives (cf. Mencius 7A/36 夫非盡人之子與 "Are not all sons of men?").

In verbal sentences the three external distributives all refer backward, to the subject or to an exposed element. Unlike the nominal sentence the verbal sentence with such a distributive can have a single subject referring to the things associated in the action:

B 22 其體俱然

"All its members are so."

A 74 是不俱當．不俱當，必或不當.

"These do not both fit the object. If they do not both fit, necessarily one does not fit."

B 48 取去俱能之....

"If he is able both to choose and to discard....."

B 67 或可或不可

"In one case it is admissible, in the other not."

B 80 莫長於是

"Nothing is longer than this."

Occasionally chü is translatable by "together", but only when association
is implied by the assertion (A 87 俱處於室　　　　"Both live in
the house/they live together in the house"). Even in a case where one
might seem to recognise the pattern "X yü Y chü..." ("X does....to-
gether with Y") the yü 與　　is simply the conjunction and the chü is
independent: A 67 （樞）尺與尺俱不盡,端與端
俱盡,尺與〈端〉或盡或不盡.

("Coinciding) Of measured feet, neither is completely covered; of start-
ing-points, both are completely covered; of foot and starting-point, one
is completely covered and the other is not."

When phrases with huo are paired the second huo is twice missing:

A 46 或去存　　　　"One is removed, the other remains."

B 11 或復否　　　　"In one case repeated, in the other not."

But in both cases the cause is probably textual corruption. In A 74 also
the second huo in a pair of phrases is missing in the editions of Pi Yüan
and Sun Yi-jang, but survived in all older editions collated by Wu Yü-

chiang. (Cf. also <u>Mo-tzu</u> ch. 48, Sun 284/6 或仁或不仁 "One was benevolent and the other not": the second <u>huo</u> is missing from a parallel in the previous line.)

In several cases <u>huo</u> and <u>mo</u> seem to refer to place ("somewhere, nowhere"). This is a curious usage, and editors have generally followed Sun Yi-jang in taking the graph 或 in such contexts to represent <u>yü</u> 域 "region". But this ignores the parallel use of <u>mo</u>:

A 42 「窮」, 或有 (=又) 前不容尺也.
或不容尺, 有窮. 莫不容尺, 無窮也.

<u>Canon</u> "A 'limit' is where, if you advance again in some direction, there is no room for the foot-rule."

<u>Explanation</u> "If in some direction there is no room for the foot-rule, it is limited; if in every direction there is room for the foot-rule, it is limitless."

A 49 「動」, 或徙也.

"To 'move' is to shift in one or other direction." (Cf. also B 13, 33.)

A 65 「盈」, 莫不有也

"To 'fill' is to be nowhere absent."

Proceeding to the internal distributives we find that their function changes according to whether the verb is transitive or intransitive. When it is intransitive they may like the external distributives refer back to the subject, but to parts of a thing or to instances of something inherently uncountable (言 "saying"):

苟是石也白, 敗是石也, 盡與白同.

"If this stone is white, when you break up this stone it is everywhere the same as the white thing."

A 60 二尺與尺, *俱去一端, 是無同也.

"When you make separate measured feet into two feet both leave one starting-point, which is being nowhere the same."

A 99 正無非 ..... 若員無直

"The exact nowhere is not...... For example, a circle is nowhere straight."

A 98 有非而不非

"in some respects is not but is not not"

The last (from an Illustration) is the only example of yu in this constru-tion. In general the Mohist assumption is that things either are or are not the same or black or straight; we can say that they are in all or no respects so, but as soon as a choice arises attention shifts to the parts or respects "by means of which" (yi 以) the things as wholes are to be judged so or not so:

A 97 以人之有黑者有不黑者也止「黑人」

"By means of what is black or what is not black in a man fixing 'black man'."

A 86, 87 有以同,「類」同也 ... 不有同,「不類」也

"Having respects in which they are the same is being of the same kind...
Not having respects in which they are the same is not being of a kind."

(The first three words are more literally "Having something by means of which they are (judged to be) the same".)

Hsiao-ch'ü NO 12　夫 物 有 以 同 而 不 率 遂 同

"Things have respects in which they are the same but it does not follow that in all respects they are the same." (This is the unique instance of shuai 率 as a distributive.)

A 68　有 以 相 攖 , 有 不 相 攖

"one part coinciding and the other part not"

It may be noted that the yi is dropped in the negative, but that yu is negated by pu (A 87) instead of being replaced by wu.

When there is no reference to the subject yu and wu in front of an intransitive verb generalise the action of the verb and convey that there are or are not circumstances in which it occurs:

B 30　買 無 貴 … 王 刀 無 變 , 糴 有 變 … .

"In no circumstances is buying at too high a price.... If the royal coin does not change from year to year but the harvest does change...."

B 35　謂 辯 無 勝

"Saying that in no circumstances does one win in disputation...."

The technical terms wu hou 無 厚 "In no circumstances thick" (dimensionless) and wu chiu 無 久 "in no circumstances long" (durationless), used of the point and the moment, presumably imply comparison; there is no thing than which the wu hou is thicker, no time than which the wu chiu is longer. This agrees with the definition of hou

(A 55 「厚」,有所大也　　　"'Dimensioned' is having some-

thing than which it is bigger" cf. (p. 119).

When on the other hand yu and wu precede a transitive verb the reference

is forward, to an implicit object:

A 4	有求	"seek something"
A 23	無知	"not know anything"
A 25	無欲惡	"not desire or dislike anything"
A 65	無盈	"not fill anything"
B 25	無加	"not put anything on top"
B 38	有指	"point something out"
B 66	無有	"not have any"
B 71	有可	"allow something"

We do not find chin "all" with a similar function, instead a double negat-

ive with wu:

B 36　　無不讓

"There is nothing he will not yield."

(Contrast the backward reference of the external distributive mo:

A 43　莫不然　　　"None are not so".)

With chin the transitive verb may be followed by an object, with yu and

wu by a directive with the preposition yü:

B 74　盡問人,則盡愛其所問.

"If he asks about all men, one loves all whom he asks about."

A 97 　有愛於人, 有不愛於人.

"love some men, not love other men"

Hsiao-ch'ü 　周乘馬 .... 有乘於馬

"ride all horses without exception. . . . . ride some horses"

Ta-ch'ü NO 2 有有於秦馬, 有有於馬也

"To have some Ch'in horses is to have some horses."

EC 11 　無貴 (=遺) 於人

"leave out no men"

A 75 　無遺於其害也

"overlook none of the harm in it".

The directive "yü X" may be taken as literally "among X" (A 97 "love some among men"). "X" may in fact be a numeral, and to enforce a contrast the directive may be preposed and resumed by yen in one case and placed in the main verbal position in the other:

B 37, 38 (contrasted Canons) 於一有知焉, 有不知焉.
. . . .有指, 於二而不可逃

"In one thing you know some of it and do not know some of it . . . . . Pointing out something is inescapably from two."

The difference of behaviour between chin and yu/wu is not of course limited to the use of an object with the former and directive with the latter. Chin is primarily the verb "to use up, expend" (B 26 上者 權重盡, 則遂 (=墜)　　　"When the leverage and weight of

the one above are spent it falls to the ground".) In more typical Mohist
contexts "X chin Y" implies that X comes to the end of Y, that Y is completely included in X. This is especially clear in the geometrical description in A 67 just quoted, but is also relevant to logical passages; the
usages in the following two examples throw light on each other:

B 65 方 貌 盡 , 俱 有 法 而 異 ....

盡 貌 , 猶 方 方 也 , 物 俱 然 .

"(Of something being so of different things) Things in which the characteristics of the square are complete all have the standard but are different.... If they have all the characteristics, as in being square, all the
things are so."

B 1 止 類 .... B 2 *止「大小」,「物盡」.... 謂 四 足 ,
「獸」與 ,「生」「鳥」與 ,「物盡」與「大小」也 .

"Fixing the class.....Fixing a wider or a narrower, or the things all included.... If you say it has four feet, is it 'animal'? Or 'the living', or
'bird'? --- 'the things all included' and 'a wider or a narrower'."
When chin is used in connexion with a transitive verb it implies that the
action comes to the end of Y, applies to all of Y. Chin may precede the
verb in the position of the other distributives, as already noticed

(盡 問 人 "ask about all men"). But if it is the chin rather than the
verb which is syntactically prominent it will itself become the main verb,
with the other verbal phrase nominalised as its subject. In the following

example the whole clause is in its turn nominalised as object of the verb

chih 智 (=知) "know":

B 74 二 智 其 數, 惡 智 ([愛民] 之 盡 *之 也)

[若] 不 智 其 數 而 智 ([愛] 之 盡 *之 也)

"Of two we know the number: how do we know that love of mankind applies

to both of them?......Like not knowing their number but knowing that

love is for all of them."

In translation a Chinese verb preceded by yu/wu is often conveniently re-

presented by an English abstract noun (A 23 "without consciousness",

A 25 "without desires and dislikes", B 30 "there is/is no change", B 35

"there is no victory"). We have deliberately avoided such equivalents in

order not to commit ourselves to the position that the Chinese verb after

yu/wu is nominalised. But certainly there are verbal units after yu/wu

which are nominalised without quantification, and some are followed by

directives. This raises the question whether there are ambiguities in the

forward-referring devices which might hinder thought on quantification.

The following are all the examples I have noticed of comparable sentences

which do not quantify. When collated they reveal certain very striking

features: wu is always written with the graph 毋 , in the single case

where we should expect yu we find huo che 或者 , the preposition is

not yü but hu 乎 . We underline the nominalised verbal unit after wu:

B 43 五 行 毋 常 勝

"There are no constant ascendancies among the five elements." (Contrast

94

B 35 謂辯無勝　　　　　　"Saying that in disputation in no case

does one win".)

B 60　　毋與非半

"There is nothing which when combined with it is not half." (This is the

interpretation which fits the context; with the standard graph for _wu_ it

would presumably be "without anything combined with it it is not half",

which would, however, require a final _yeh_ cf. p. 80).

B 72　謂者毋「惟」乎其謂

"The speaker has no 'is and only is' for what he calls it." (The word

wei 'is and only is' seems to be quoted from the Canon cf. p. 103).

B 74　或者遺乎其問也

"Some are left out of his question." (Cf. the examples of 無遺於 ....

in A 75, EC 11, quoted above. 有遺於其問　　　would presum-

ably be "leaves out some that he asked about".)

Ta-ch'ü EC 10　興利有厚薄而毋倫列之〈謂〉
　　　　　　　興利為己

"Beneficial action in which one does more for some and less for others,

but without grading according to relationships, is what is called 'bene-

ficial action with a selfish motive'." (Not "in no case grading according

to relationships"; the motive would be selfish whenever one fails to do so.)

Hsiao-ch'ü NO 14,15 心毋空乎內

"The heart has no hollow inside it."

If we proceed to look for other examples of the graph 囟 , we find

none except for a single case of the negative imperative wu (B 38). The

only other example of the preposition hu immediately follows the sentence

quoted from B 72, and seems from the parallelism to be a scribal error

(彼 循 惟 [手] 其 謂 .... 彼 苦 不 惟 其 謂

"If the other still is and only is what it is called. . . . If the other is not

only what it is called. . . .")

It would seem then that the Mohist dialecticians deliberately reserved the

pre-verbal yu/wu for quantification, and avoided the confusion which

might result from their use in other constructions by choosing other

graphs and particles.

Another possible difficulty in quantification by yu and wu would be the

quantification of yu and wu themselves. Of the four theoretical possibilities

(yu yu "have some", yu wu "lack some", wu yu "have none", wu wu "lack

none") the second would be ambiguous, since yu and wu might be taken as

co-ordinate, "having and lacking", We do in fact find two passages where

yu wu might be expected, and in both it is avoided. In one the yu is ab-

sent from a theoretically possible yu wu yen:

B 49 若 無 焉 , 則 有 之 而 后 無 .

"In the case of there not being some of something, there is not only after

there was."

In the other the theoretically possible 欲 有 無 "wish to be without some" is replaced by a construction with huo che:

B 44　或者欲不有

"wish that you did not have some".

Thus both of the examples of huo che in the corpus (B 44, 74) serve to

avoid difficulties in quantifying with yu.

Of the three unambiguous combinations, there is no example of wu wu or

a substitute. But we find not only wu yu (B 66 不偏有偏無有

"They do not in one case have and in the other not have any") but an extra-

ordinary example of yu yu with a directive, assumed by previous editors

to be corrupt:

Ta-ch'ü NO 2　有有於秦馬有有於馬也

"To have some Ch'in horses is to have some horses."

It will be seen that there is no need to emend this sentence. From the

point of view of style, elegance means nothing to the Mohist, syntactic

clarity means everything; and within his system the sentence is unam-

biguous.

Among the interrogative pronouns shu 孰　and shui 誰　"which"

are close in behaviour to the external and internal distributives respect-

ively. The former refers back to the subject, of which there may be

more than one:

B 6　木與夜孰長

"Which is longer, a tree or a night?"

We commonly think of shui as referring exclusively to persons ("who?").
But since a person is an individual picked out by the question there is a
close connexion between words translatable as "which?" and as "who?";
in other texts shu often refers to persons and shui sometimes to things.
The following example is from elsewhere in Mo-tzu:

ch. 47 (Sun 264/6) 「駕驥與羊，子將誰歐」....
「將歐驥也」

'With either thoroughbreds or sheep to yoke to your carriage, which
would you drive?' .... 'I would drive thoroughbreds'".
In the same chapter we find a construction comparable to the "yu/wu-
verb-yü X" pattern discussed above:

ch. 46 (Sun 268/10) 子誰貴於此二人．

"Of these two men which will you honour?"

The dialectical chapters contain three examples of shui:

B 41 不知其誰謂也

(Canon) "not know which he refers to", a question rephrased in the Explanation as 何謂也 "What does it refer to?".

B 44 誰愛

"Who would one love?"

B 70 猶白若黑也，誰勝

"For example, it is white or it is black, with which answer does one
win?"

In the first two shui as object is comparable with shu as subject. In the

last case it is possible to translate simply "Who wins?". But the sym-
metry with the distributives suggest rather that it should be assimulated
to the <u>wu</u> of B 35 辯 無 勝 ("In disputation in no circumstances
does one win"),"in which circumstances does one win?". We may note
also that with the addition of <u>shu</u> and <u>shui</u> three of the four pairs of distributives show a phonological similarity:

<u>huo</u>/ * G'WəK   <u>yu</u>/ * GĬUG

<u>mo</u>/ * MÂK   <u>wu</u>/ * MĬWO

<u>shu</u>/ * D̂ĬÔK   <u>shui</u>/ * D̂ĬWəR

This suggests that the Mohists conceived the three external distributives
as the internal distributives modified by a final -K. It may be added that
<u>ko</u> 各 /*KLÂK "each", which occupies the same pre-verbal position
and has the same final -K, is not used in the dialectical chapters (nor is
<u>mei</u> 每 "each").

Questions

The interrogative particle <u>hu</u> 乎 , used after verbal sentences, appears
once (B 41). <u>Yü</u> 與 , the interrogative form of final <u>yeh</u>, appears
five times (B 2, 10, 39). In three cases it follows nominal units; in one
case where it follows a verbal clause belonging to the type 1C elsewhere
defined (p. 136 "It is that.....") both <u>yeh</u> and <u>yü</u> are present:

B 10 智 與, 以 己 為 然 也 與 .

"Is it knowing? Or is it that one supposes to be so what is already past?"

Since so many questions are about the alternatives of disputation the

commonest interrogative pronouns are shu 孰 and shui 誰 "which?"

the former referring backward and the latter forward. These are more

conveniently discussed with the distributives (p. 97-99). The other inter-

rogative pronouns are ho 何 (object: "what?") and wu 惡 (direct-

ive: "to, in, from what?"). In two passages they can be seen to be in

correspondence with object chih and directive yen:

B 41 「飄何謂也」. 彼曰, 「飄施」則智之

"'What does X refer to?' If he says 'An X is a Y' then one does know

it."

B 38 是智是之不智也. 惡得為一謂而
有智焉, 有不智焉.

"This would be knowing the very thing one does not know, and in what can

it be supposed that, the reference being to a single thing, there is some-

thing one knows in it and something one does not?"

Wu appears also in the phrases 惡可存 (B 42 "Where may it

be kept?") and 惡智 (B 74 "Whence does one know..... ?"). The

latter is conveniently translated "How does one know..... ?", but there

is no reason to assume that the common pre-Han practice of asking this

question with wu or with an 安 "where " implies any weakening of

the directive function. (Cf. the question "Whence (an) do you know that

the fish are happy?", which Chuang-tzu derided by the answer "I know it
from up above the Hao"[6].)

It is remarkable that there are no interrogative adverbs in the Canons
and Explanations. But in the Hsiao-ch'ü we find an explanation (not a use)
of ch'i 豈 , rhetorical "How....?" implying the answer "No", and
two adverbial combinations with hsi 奚 (我奚獨不可以然也
"Why should it not be so in my case too?", 奚以明之   "By
what means shall we make it clear?").

Quotation

The particle combination yeh che 也者   is equivalent to "unquote",
implying that what is under discussion is the meaning of the preceding
word or phrase. In the Hsiao-ch'ü it marks technical terms introduced
for definition (「或」也者不盡也 "Some is not all"). In the Explanations its function seems at first sight to be the same, since in the earlier
examples the word so treated is in fact the term defined in the Canon
(A 3-6, 32). But throughout the first four the sentences lack the final yeh
of definitions; and on closer inspection one sees that every one of the 11
single words followed by yeh che is a direct quotation from the corresponding Canon (A 3-6, 32, 46, 64, 71, 83, B 31, 35). Even when there
is a definition it is of the word as used in the context of the Canon (cf.
A 46, 71, B 31). In A 83, in a series of three explanations of terms, the

only yeh che is after the second, the one which is from the Canon:

A 83 *可者，用而勿必．「必」也者，可〈而〉
勿疑．*假者，兩而勿偏．

"The allowable, employ but do not treat as necessary; the "necessary",
allow and do not doubt: arguments which reverse, present as a pair, do
not present one without the other."

The yeh che phrase always stands at the head of the sentence. Much more
common is the quoted word or phrase attached to the end of the sentence
by yeh. This device is used systematically in A 76-89, B 2, 3, 9, 10,
42, 58, but also occurs in isolated sentences elsewhere (B 27?, 29?, 36,
55, 61-64, 66, 70). It accounts for a number of apparently clumsy sentences in which what might conveniently have been treated as subject
stands at the end:

B 63 區不可偏擧，「*宇」也．

" If a bounded area cannot be presented apart from what bounds it, it is
(what the Canon means by) 'space'."

In three cases yeh che follows a unit of more than one word:

Hsiao-ch'ü NO 6 「是猶謂」也者，同也．「吾豈謂」也者，異也

"'This is like saying....' implies similarity, 'How can I say...?' implies difference."

A 78 命之「馬」，「類」也．「若實」也者，必以
是名也．

"When one names it 'horse', it is the 'class'. For 'like the object' one necessarily uses this name." (Cf. also A 31.)

In the last case it is tempting to emend, omitting the yeh: "For what is like the object one necessarily uses this name". But there seems to be no objection to retaining it, in which case the Mohist is making the much more sophisticated assertion that a class name is an abbreviation of "a thing like the individual X".

It will be noticed that yeh che serves as a quotation device only when the meaning of the word or phrase is itself the topic of discussion. In the dialectical chapters the unit "X yeh che" is always at the head of the sentence, followed by either a defining "Y yeh" phrase or an explanatory clause without yeh. The absence of unrestricted quotation devices in the text as we have it (in the original text there may of course have been graphic devices) often leaves us in serious doubt as to whether the Mohist is concerned with the word itself or what it refers to, or even whether he is himself clear about the distinction:

B 33 「或」,過名也.

"The 'huo' is a name which lapses" (apparently about the phrase huo hsi 或從 , cf. p. 88).

B 72 「惟吾謂」,非名也則不可

.... 謂者毋「惟」乎其謂

Canon "'It is and only is what I call it' is inadmissible unless it is its name."

103

Explanation ".....The speaker has no 'is and only is' for what it is called."

Particles with logical functions

The Canons and Explanations have two conjunctions of implication, tse 則 "(if...) then" indicating that B follows from A, and erh hou 而後(后)"only then" indicating that A is a necessary condition of B.

B 70 聞 所 不 知 若 所 知, 則 兩 知 之.

"If you hear that something you do not know is like something you do know you know them both."

A 1 「故」, 所 得 而 後 成 也.

"A 'cause' is what must be got before it will come about."

The adverb pi 必 "certainly, necessarily" appears only in clause B in the case of tse, only in clause A in the case of erh hou:

B 25 兩 加 焉 重 相 若, 則 標 必 下.

"If you put equal weights on both of them the tip is certain to decline"

(cf. also B 48, Ta-ch'ü NO 10).

B 64 行 者 必 先 近 而 後 遠.

"The traveller is necessarily at first nearer and only afterwards farther away" (cf. also B 8, 51).

Pi in the second of successive verbal phrases always implies that B is the consequence of A, whether tse is present or not:

B 25 　加重於其一旁必垂

"If you put a weight on one side of it it is certain to decline."

This allows a very economical way of putting one implication inside another:

B 2 　此然是必然則俱為麋

"Granted that if it is so of the thing here it is necessarily so of what the thing is judged to be, then both will be milu deer."

The essential function of <u>tse</u> is to authorise inference from A to B; the sentence may itself make the inference (B 73 　有窮則可盡

"If it is limited it is exhaustible") but more often, as is especially clear in the passage on mechanics just quoted (B 25), entitles us to infer B when we encounter A. The logical relationship is allowed to weaken only in a few cases of parallel clauses which merely contrast what happens in contrasted conditions:

B 10 　舉之則輕,廢之則重,非有力也

"A case where if he lifts something it is light and if he puts it down it is heavy is not a test of strength" (cf. also B 35, discussed p. 137, B 49).

The strictness of the implication when <u>tse</u> is used in formal argument can be seen from this example:

<u>Hsiao-ch'ü</u> NO 17 　之馬之目 *眇, 則 *謂之馬 *眇.
　　　　　　　　之馬之目大, 而不謂之馬大.

"If this horse's eyes are blind we say that this horse is blind; when this horse's eyes are big we do not say that this horse is big."

105

In this pair of sentences (and in two other pairs in the same series) <u>tse</u> in the first is replaced by <u>erh</u> in the second, because we cannot infer that a horse with big eyes is not big. In English we can tolerate "if" in both sentences, and indeed I used the word in both in a previously published translation of the <u>Hsiao-ch'ü</u>. [7)]

<u>Jo</u> 若 "if" is absent from the <u>Canons</u> and appears only nine times in the <u>Explanations</u>, in all but two cases merely marking the beginning of the A clause or clauses before <u>tse</u>. The <u>Ta-ch'ü</u> uses it only at the head of one sentence, where it may be a mistake for the <u>chu</u> 諸 of a parallel sentence (EC 1). The <u>Ta-ch'ü</u> is unique in using <u>tse</u> only once and employing both <u>kou</u> 苟 "if" (which would have the advantage of being clearly distinguished from the very common <u>jo</u> "like") and the contra-factual <u>chieh</u> "supposing that":

EC 6 苟不智其所在

"If you do not know where he is" (cf. NO 1).

EC 4 藉臧也死而天下害,吾特養臧也萬倍.

"Supposing that if Jack died the world would be harmed, my special care for Jack would be a myriadfold."

The <u>Hsiao-ch'ü</u> uses <u>tse</u> freely, but <u>jo</u> only twice in the formula (itself a reminder of the advantages of <u>kou</u>) 若若是則.... "if it is like this, then...."

In the <u>Ta-ch'ü</u> and <u>Hsiao-ch'ü</u> we find <u>jan hou</u>/* NIAN G'U in addition to

erh hou/*NIə GG'U "only then". Since both are combinations of two words,
or at any rate treated as such in writing, we need not regard this innovation
as the arbitrary introduction of a synonym; the purpose of the slight variation was perhaps to contrast the A clause by jan and the B clause by erh,
as is suggested by a passage in the Hsiao-ch'ü which uses both (No 16).
Of more interest is a single instance of the rare conjunction yen. This
seems at first sight to be synonymous with crh hou and jan hou, as it is
elsewhere in Mo-tzu:

Mo-tzu ch. 14 (Sun 65/1) 必知亂之所自起，焉能治
之．不知亂之所自起，則不能治．

"He must know the source of disorder before he will be able to reduce it
to order; if he does not know the source he will not be able to reduce it
to order."

But it appears that the word was still recognised as related to final ycn,
and that its basic sense was "only in it":

ch. 46 (Sun 271/10) 夫倍義而鄉祿者，我常聞之矣．
倍祿而鄉義者，於高石子焉見之也．

"I have often heard of men who did an about-face from duty to salary;
only in Kao Shih tzu have I seen a man who did an about-face from salary
to duty."

We can be sure that a Mohist dialectician would not introduce a new word
into his restricted stock of particles unless it had a unique function:

Ta-ch'ü NO 2 以 形 貌 命 者, 必 智 是 之 某 也, 焉 智 某 也.

"With those which name according to shape and features it is necessary to know that this thing is "X", it is only in it that one knows X."

(Cf. B 38 惡 得 為 一 謂 而 有 智 焉, 有 不 智 焉.

"In what can it be supposed that, the reference being to a single thing, there is something one knows in it and something one does not?")

A tendency for the Ta-ch'ü and Hsiao-ch'ü to elaborate and refine the terminology of implication is also visible in their use of adverbial yin 因 "on these grounds" in addition to ku 故 "therefore". While ku is primarily a noun ("reason", on the evidence of its phonetic and graphic relation to ku 古 "ancient times" basically "what is at its origins"), yin is primarily a verb, "take as basis for doing something" (cf. Ta-ch'ü EC 1). It appears in the Canons as a noun, the "grounds" or "criterion" of a judgment (A 98, B 3, 15), clearly distinguished from ku, which is used of reasons in general but in particular for causes (cf. A 1, 77). Adverbially also it refers to the grounds of a judgment, not the cause of an event:

Hsiao-ch'ü No 16 乘 馬 〈不〉 待 周 乘 馬 然 後 乘 馬 也, 有 乘 於 馬 因 為 乘 馬 矣

"If he has ridden some horses, on these grounds he is deemed to ride horses" (more idiomatically, to bring out the force of the yi, "these are sufficient grounds for him to be deemed to ride horses"). Cf. also

Ta-ch'ü NO 2

Besides the conjunctive yü 與　　"and", used between nominal units
which may be of some length (cf. A 97, B 10), there is a disjunctive particle jo 若　　"or". The two examples (B 10, 70) are quoted elsewhere (p. 98, 123). The disjunctive jo, very rare in other texts, appears
about 50 times in the military chapters of Mo-tzu, in instructions for
defence allowing for alternative possibilities. It may intervene between
either nominal or verbal units, which may be single words or clauses of
considerable length:

Ts'en 105/5　　朝 夕 立 若 坐

"morning and evening stand or sit"

56/2　　置 康 若 炭 其 中

"put chaff or ashes inside"

109/9　　非 其 分 職 而 擅 取 之 , 若 非 其 所 常
　　　　治 而 擅 為 之 , 斷 .

"If without authority he takes over what is not his allotted office, or without authority deals with matters which are not his business, he is to be
sentenced."

55/13　　適 (=敵) 人 為 變 , 築 垣 聚 土 非 常 者 , 若
　　　　彭 (=旁) 有 水 湣 非 常 者 , 此 穴 土 也 .

"The enemy behaving differently, building walls or piling earth in an unusual way, or an unusual amount of water at the side, are signs of tunneling."

Comparison

The standard word to express similarity is the verb jo 若 "like". We class it as a verb because it occupies a verbal position in the sentence and is negatable by pu 不 (unlike the particles jo "if" and jo "or"). As the introductory word in the formula of the Illustrations it is used very loosely and is often conveniently translated by "for example. ...". On the other hand where degrees are being compared it has a very precise sense, "as much as" (B 25 權重相若 "They are equal in leverage and in weight"). In ordinary pre-Han usage jo is negatable only when degree is implied (pu jo "not as much as, not as good as"), but in the dialectical chapters there is a complete assimilation of negative to positive usage (pu jo "not like", A 7, 11, 74, B 3, 81). We find this also in a passage in the Lü-shih ch'un-ch'iu which seems to reflect the in-fluence of the dialecticians:

ch. 23, part 5 (Hsü 23/14A/2) 牛之性不若羊‚羊之性不若豕

"The ox's nature is not like the sheep's, the sheep's nature is not like the pig's."

Jo in front of an exposed element at the head of the sentence ("With re-gard to. ...") is found only in the combination jo fu 若夫 (B 27). We do, however, find jo in front of the verb ("as though, seems"):

B 22   多而若少

"There is more but seems to be less" (cf. also A 99, B 38).

Yu 猶 is not negatable, and must therefore be classed not as a verb but as a particle, used in the pattern "(X) yu Y". "(With X) it is as with Y". It does not like jo imply a general similarity between X and Y, but introduces Y as a clearer example to which the specific observation being made about X will more easily be seen to apply:

B 66 是狂舉也．猶牛有齒馬有尾．

"This is picking indiscriminately, as with 'Oxen have teeth but horses have tails'" (as evidence that an ox is not a horse).

The contrast between jo and yu can be seen in this example (which also has the disjunctive jo "or"):

B 70 是所不智若所智也．猶「白」若「黑」也．
誰勝．是若其色也．若白者必白....

"This implies that the unknown thing is like something we do know. For example, 'It is white' or 'It is black', with which will the disputant win? This is like its colour, what is like white is necessarily white....."

In two cases a phrase with yu seems to be parenthetic:

B 65 或木或石．不害其方之相*合也．
盡貌，猶方也，物俱然．

(On things which share one standard all being 'so') "Some are wood and some stone, but it does not affect their agreement in being square. If they have all the characteristics, as in the case of being square, all of the things are so." (Not "If in all characteristics they are like the square..")

A 32 謂言．猶石．致也．

111

"To speak calling by name, as in the case of the stone, is to communicate" (?) (However we understand this obscure sentence, we cannot take it
to be comparing some other object with a stone.)

For the other examples of "(X) yu Y", cf. A 75, B 8, 27, 60, 78, Hsiao-
ch'ü NO 6.

The temporal adverb yu "still" is probably a derivative of the conjunction
("as before, as it was"). We find it both as a single word (A 75, B 72,
Ta-ch'ü EC 2) and in combinations which appear to be transitional between conjunction and adverb, yu shih yeh 猶是也 "as it was" as
complement of the sentence (B 50) and adverbial yu chih 猶之 (B 72).
The latter is syntactically remarkable since it treats yu as verbal. Both
combinations are common in other pre-Han texts:

Mo-tzu ch. 47 (Sun 281/4) 是猶以卵投石也．盡天下
之卵，其石猶是也，不可毀也

"This is as with throwing eggs at a stone. After throwing all the eggs in
the world the stone is still as it was; it cannot be broken." (Cf. Mencius
4B/28, 6A/2.)

Kuan-tzu ch. 64 故雖地小而民少，猶之為天子
也．．．．故雖地大民眾，猶之困辱而死亡也

"Therefore although his land was small and people few, he still became
Emperor..... Therefore although their lands were great and people many
they still perished in misery and disgrace."

Numerals

The numeral may stand in a nominal position (B 59 "Five has one in it").

But in the main sentence position it is verbal, without final yeh and negat-

ed and distributed by the pu 不 and chü 俱 which precede the

verb, not the fei 非 and chieh 皆 which precede the comple-

ment:

B 3　　俱鬥,不俱二　　　"They both fight, they are not both

　　　　　　　　　　　　　two"

B 7, 12　俱一　　　　　　"They are both one"

B 12　　牛馬二　　　　　　"An ox and a horse are two"

B 18　　景二　　　　　　　"The shadows are two/there are two

　　　　　　　　　　　　　shadows"

Numeral adjunct with head may stand in a nominal position (B 18

二光夾一光 "Two lights flank one light"). But in a verbal position

it functions verbally, without the addition of a verb such as yu 有

"there is":

A 39　二人而俱見是　　"They are two men and both see that

　　　楹也　　　　　　this is a pillar"

A 86　二名一實　　　　"There are two names but one object"

B 12　牛馬四足　　　　"Ox and horse have four feet"

B 18　一光者　　　　　"That which has one light"

Ta-ch'ü No 7　一貌者　　　"Things one in appearance"

Hsiao-ch'ü No 17 二馬而或白 "There are two horses and one is

　　　　　　　　　　　　　white"

Yi 矣

Except for the interrogative particles and yeh the only final particle is

yi, which marks the point of transition from one state to the next in the

manner of colloquial le 了 . It appears only six times, and in each of

them the transition point is easily recognised: A 28 吾事治矣

"Once our affairs have reached the point of being properly ordered";

A 99 有説過五(=伍)諾,無説用五諾,若自然矣.

(On agreeing that something is circular when it perfectly matches a

circle) "When after argument you assent to more than the matching, or

without argument assent on the evidence of the matching, it has become

as though it were so of itself."

B 26 權重相若則*止矣. "When the leverage and weight of the

two have equalised they come to a stop"; Hsiao-ch'ü NO 14 若若是

..... 則無難矣 "If it is like this (with A, B, C....)..... then

there will no longer be any difficulty (about X, Y, Z)". In two cases the

transition point has been described as "awaited" (待) in an earlier

phrase:

Ta-ch'ü NO 10 ...其困也可立而待也. ...則必困矣.

"If......., he can be expected to get into trouble at any moment. If....,

then he will certainly get into trouble."

Hsiao-ch'ü NO 16 「不愛人」不待周不愛人,不[失]周愛因為不愛人矣.

"'He does not love men' does not require him to (literally 'wait for him to') love no men at all; he does not love men without exception, on these grounds he is deemed not to love men." (Here we could bring out the effect of yi by inserting "it is sufficient that" after the semi-colon.)

Wei 謂

Uses of the verb wei "call" fall into three patterns:

Pattern 1: wei with two objects, the first a pronoun and the second a noun:

A 74　或謂之「牛」，　　　"One calls it 'ox', the other 'non-
　　　謂之「非牛」　　　ox'" (Cf. the immediately preceding

　　　　　　　　　　　A 73　「凡牛」「#區非牛」，兩也

　　　　　　　　　　　"'All oxen' and 'non-oxen as a group'

　　　　　　　　　　　is presenting as a pair".)

B 33　謂此「南方」　　　"Call this place 'the South'"

B 72　謂是「霍」　　　　"Call the said thing 'crane'"

Pattern 2: wei before a verbal clause with subject and verb:

A 46　謂其存者損　　　"Say that what remains of it is re-
　　　　　　　　　　　duced"

B 35　謂辯無勝　　　　"Say that there is no winner in dis-
　　　　　　　　　　　putation"

Pattern 3: wei before an "X is Y" clause with subject and complement:

B 72　謂彼是是也　　　"Say that that and this are both this"

115

The last is the sole instance of its pattern, but the presence of a final yeh clearly distinguishes it from Pattern 1.

It may be objected that the last two patterns might be reduced to Pattern 1 by identifying the noun after wei as object and not as subject. The distinction between English "call...." and "say that...." would then be merely a convenience of translation. Is it perhaps artificial to refuse to treat the first example of Pattern 1 as "One says that it is an ox, the other that it is not an ox" or of Pattern 2 as "Call what remains of it 'reduced'"? However, it does not seem artificial to insist on the difference in such a case as B 54 謂之「殺犬」 "call it 'killing a dog'" (not "say that he killed a dog"). The patterns could be reduced to one only if the pronoun object chih were always substitutable for the noun after wei. But in this as in other pre-Han texts wei chih is followed only by the limited variety of words and phrases which are acceptable as appellations.

In Pattern 1 the second object may be dropped; the pronoun object continues to indicate what is referred to, not what it is called:

B 3　而後謂之　　　　　　　"only then does one refer to it"

謂是...謂也 (=他)　　　"refer to this one..... refer to an-

　　　　　　　　　　　　　other one"

B 41　其誰謂也　　　　　　"which thing he refers to"

何謂也　　　　　　　　　"What does it refer to?"

116

A 80, B 35, 49 所謂   "What it refers to" (cf. A 80

所以謂,名也. 所謂,
實也.

"What one uses to refer is the name,

that to which one refers is the ob-

ject").

As in other pre-Han texts, the presence or absence of final yeh is sig-

nificant when a single unit after wei is not a pronoun:

B 2   謂四足   "say it has four feet"

A 62 (cf. 51, 63, 64)

謂夾之者也   "refers to those which flank it"

The patterns without and with yeh may be treated as Patterns 2 and 3 with

the subject dropped.

When wei stands alone it indicates the applying of name to object or a

name which is being applied to an object; the two senses are not clearly

distinguished:

B 72   吾謂   "what I call it"

其謂   "what it is called"

謂者   "the man applying the name"

B 38   一謂   "the applying of one name"

B 3   無謂   "there is no applying of the name" (the con-

text forbids "does not refer to anything").

The familiar constructions "X 之謂   Y" ("It is X that is meant by Y")

117

and "X 之謂也" ("It is X that is referred to") appear in the Ta-ch'ü but not apparently in the Canons and Explanations (cf. however A 21).

Che 者

Except in hsi che 昔者 "yesterday" (EP 2) and at the end of phrases containing so, the particle che stands exclusively after nominalised verbal units. In subjectless phrases the reference appears to be exclusively to the agent, although there may be cases where one may hesitate to insist on this point (cf. A 7 愛己者非為用己也 "With the man who loves himself, it is not for the sake of the use to which he puts himself"). In A 83 and again at the beginning of the Hsiao-ch'ü we find defined verbal terms ending in yeh che mixed with apparently similar words followed by che alone, but in each case the difference emerges on closer inspection.

That che can be assumed to mark the agent of a preceding verb and not merely to nominalise it is significant for the analysis of many obscure phrases:

A 98   然者...不然者   "what is so....what is not so"

A 51   一然者,一不然者   "a thing in one respect so, a thing in one respect not so"

B 65   一法者   "things sharing one standard"

B 17   一光...一光者   "one light....what is under one light"

B 22-24	鑒....鑒者	"the mirror.... the man looking at himself in the mirror"
B 27	沇(=流)埞者	"what makes the ladder glide"
B 68	正名者	"one who uses names correctly"
A 31	若名者	"what is like the name"
B 70	若白者	"what is like the white"

In the Ta-ch'ü we find long phrases in the pattern chu....che, using the collective prefix chu 諸 confined in the Canons and Explanations to the phrase 諸口 "speakers in general" (A 32):

NO 2 諸以居運命者

"All which name according to residence or migration."

So

In the relative pronoun we do not find the distinction between object and directive which is made in the 3rd person (chih 之 , yen 焉) and among interrogative pronouns (ho 何 , wu 惡). In this as in most other sources we do not find the combination so yü 所於 . The use of so as object followed by a transitive verb ("him whom, that which") is much the more frequent and presents no difficulty. But so as directive followed by an intransitive verb shares the ambiguity of all directive units. There is one case of so ta 所大 . Since "ta yü X" can only be "bigger than X", this seems to be unambiguous:

A 55 「厚」，有所大也. *端無所大.

"Canon 'Dimensioned' is having something than which it is bigger.

Explanation A starting-point has nothing than which it is bigger."

This is confirmed by a sentence in a well-known exposition of relativism in the "Autumn Waters" chapter of Chuang-tzu (Liu 6 下, 9 A/4): "If on the basis of something than which it is bigger you treat it as big, none of the myriad things is not big" (因其所大而大之，則萬物莫不大).

We also find two cases of so jan 所然 . We observe this also in the "Autumn Waters" passage, but in an un-Mohist usage: so jan "what he approves", parallel with so fei "what he condemns". The dialectical chapters do not use jan transitively, nor do they use intransitive jan to express approval. There is, however, a case where jan is intransitive in another relativist discourse in Chuang-tzu, (ch. 27 Liu 9 上 , 16 A/3-8 有自也而然 ..... 惡乎然 . 然於然 ..... 物固有所然 ..."There is a direction from which something is so......From what is it so? It is so from something which is so..... If a thing really has something from which it is so......."). Cf. Han Fei tzŭ ch. 20 (Ch'en 365/1) 道者萬物之所然也 "The Tao is the source wherefrom all things are so". One of the Mohist examples is evidently of this type, however we decide to interpret it:

A 70, 71 「法」，所若而然也．「佴」，所然也

"The 'standard' is that in being like which a thing is so..... The 'erh' (unidentified word) is where it is so."

120

In the other example the significance of the directive so is fixed by the preceding verb, tsai "be in" (used causatively):

B 16 在 諸 (=之於) 其 所 然 , 未 然 者

"Locating it in the time in which it is so or in the not yet so."

Yi 以

Yi serves primarily as a preposition before a nominal unit ("by means of, because of", B 48 以 名 取 "choose by means of the name") or as a conjunction between verbal units, marking the first as the means and the second as the end (A 98 止 因 以 別 道 "Fix the grounds and thereby/in order to distinguish courses"). In the latter case it is seldom material whether one decides that the yi refers back ("thereby") or that it refers forward ("in order to").

Yi also appears in the familiar combinations:

所 以	"that by means of which, that because of which"
以 為	"deem"
以 x 為 Y	"deem X to be Y"
可 以	"may....."
足 以	"is adequate to....." (followed by active verbs, the verb after 可 alone and in other texts, 足 being passive)
x 將 以	"the purpose of X is to...."
有 以 , 無 以	"have the means to, lack the means to....."

The last phrase is firmly attested only in the sense "have respects in which..., are partly": the yi is dropped when the phrase is negated:

A 68 有 以 相 攖 , 有 不 相 攖

"Partly coinciding, partly not."

A 86, 87 有 以 同 .... 不 有 同

"Having respects in which they are the same..... not having respects in which they are the same." (The former phrase also Hsiao-ch'ü NO 12.)

Yi presents problems only when it stands as the main verb of the sentence. In two cases it is equivalent to yi wei "deem""

B 47 非 以 火 之 熱 我 有

"It is not that one thinks of the heat of the fire as belonging to oneself."

B 71 以 當 必 不 審

"To suppose that it fits the fact is necessarily ill-considered."

It is possible that in both cases wei has dropped out of the text, but this usage is attested elsewhere in Mo-tzu (ch. 39 Sun 189/9 俱 以 賢 人 也 "All think him an excellent man").

In other cases the instrument with yi is all that is explicit of a clause with a dropped verb, and its significance is only plain when one recognises the type of verb:

1. Preposition yi as in A 3 「知」也者, 所 以 知 也   ("As for the 'intelligence', it is the means by which one knows").

B 46 知而不以五路

"One knows, but it is not by means of the five senses."

2. Preposition yi as in A 80 所以謂,名也 ("That by which one calls something is the name"):

A 78 「若實」也者,必以是名也.

"For 'like the object' one necessarily uses this name."

3. Preposition yi as in B 9 物之所以然 ("The reason why a thing is so").

B 10 鬪者之敝也, 以飲酒若以*日中, 是不可智也.

"Whether the fighter's collapse is because of drinking wine or because of the midday sun cannot be known."

4. Preposition yi as in " 以 X 論 Y" ("discuss X in terms of Y")

B 78 誹之可否不以眾寡.... 論誹之可不可, 以理之可誹...... 是猶以長論短.

"Whether criticisms are admissible or not is not (to be discussed) in terms of how many or how few..... In discussing whether or not criticism is admissible, if it is in terms of in principle deserving criticism.... This is like discussing the short in terms of whether it is long enough."

5. Conjunction yi, with a preceding verbal unit dropped (cf. Mo-tzu ch. 9

(Sun 40/7) 此言聖人之德，章明博大填固以
脩久也　　　"This is to say that the virtue of the sage is long-lasting in its glory, extensiveness, firmness").

B 64 行 *脩 以久 ... 民 行 脩，必 以久也

"If one travels a certain distance one does so for a certain time.....If people travel a certain distance they necessarily do so for a certain time."

A 50 　止，以久也

"To 'stop' is to be so for a certain time."

6. Preposition yi, with wei 為 Y.

B 3 為麗，不必 *其〈與類〉，不必*其與暴也
若為「夫」，〈以〉勇，不為「夫」．為屨，以「買衣」，為屨．

"Making an addition, one cannot be sure either that it will be of a kind with it or that it will conflict with it.....For example he is a fu; use yung (as the added word: 勇夫 "bold fellow") and he will not be a fu (husband). They are chü; use mai yi (for the added words: 買衣屨 "buy coat and shoes") and they will be chü (shoes)."

In the case of objectless transitive verbs the instrument with yi may either precede or follow the verb:

B 48 　以名取　　　　　"choose by means of the name"

Hsiao-ch'ü NO 10 以類取，以 "accept according to the class, pre-
類予　　　　　　　sent according to the class"

B 41 應以弗智   "answer that one does not know it"

B 44 說以少連   "show by the example of Shao-lien"

With this exception the instrumental phrase, however long and unwieldly,

precedes the verb:

A 97 以(人之有黑者,有不黑者也)止黑人

"Using what is black or what is not black in a man to fix 'black man'...."

Hsiao-ch'ü No 11 「推」也者,以(其所不取之同於其所取者)予之也

"To 'infer' is to present to him on the grounds of a similarity between

what he does not accept and something that he does accept."

A 20 以(其敢於是也)命之,不以(其不敢於彼也)害之.

"One names him ('brave') because of what he does dare, does not slander

him because of what he does not dare."

Among the examples above, in B 41 the instrument serves as secondary

object of the verb ying 應   , the immediate object of which is a per-

son (B 41 應之   "answer him"). This belongs to the elsewhere

familiar formula 以 X 與 / 告 / 示 Y "give/tell/show X to

Y". But in this case the instrument follows the verb, and it is remarkable

that there are no instances of the instrument serving as preposed object

throughout these chapters. In the two examples from the Hsiao-ch'ü just

quoted we have phrases in the form " 以 X 予 (Y)", "present to Y

using X as grounds" (not "present X to Y"); in the single example in the

125

corpus of a secondary object of this verb it follows the immediate object

(B 69 使人予人酒 "cause someone to give somebody else wine").

We may compare also B 53 以名視 (=示) 人 "show to others by

means of a name" (not "show others a name").

Erh 而

The rule that both units linked by the conjunction erh are verbal applies

universally in the Canons and Explanations. The relationship is either of

co-ordination or of subordination of the first unit to the second.

Throughout pre-Han literature the unit after erh is verbal, but inside

subordinate, embedded or auxiliary clauses the first unit is sometimes

a subject or exposed element. In the Ta-ch'ü there are cases of erh after

an exposed directive in a preliminary clause. The purpose in each case

is to contrast directives in parallel clauses.

EC 8 ((於) 所未有而取焉), 是利之中取大也.

(於 所 既有 而 棄焉), 是害之中取小也.

"Choosing between things that one does not yet have is choosing the

greater among benefits. Sacrificing one of the things that one already has

is choosing the lesser among harms." (Cf. also the contrasting defin-

itions at the beginnings of EC 7, 8.)

Yü 於

The directive preposition is yü, replaced by hu 乎 only in a special

pattern discussed elsewhere (p. 94-96). In the 3rd person there is a directive pronoun yen 焉 , equivalent to yü chih 之 (to be distinguished
from the conjunction yen "only in it", found in the Ta-ch'ü and elsewhere
in Mo-tzǔ).

In a few cases the directive unit stands in the main verbal position:

B 37, 38 (Contrasting Canons) 於 一 有 知 焉, 有 不 知 焉
....有 指, 於 二 而 不 可 逃.

"In one thing there is something he knows and something he does not
know..... Pointing out something is from two things, and this is ines-
capable."

But in this case the placing of the directive serves to bring out the contrast, and other cases are textually open to question (A 88, B 39, 53,).

There are cases of the familiar formula "X chih yü Y yeh": "X in relation
to Y":

B 44   若 (酒 之 於 人 也)

"For example the effects of wine on a man."

In this formula both related units are nominal. But in two cases long
verbal phrases seem to be linked together or with a noun. This involves
the dropping of chih, making the formula "X yü Y yeh":

B 39   若「殆 於 域 土成 門 與」, 於 臧 也.

"For example 'I suppose he is inside the city gates?', in talking of Jack."

B 57 以 *楹 為 摶, 於 以 為 無 知 也

"Judging a pillar to be round, in relation to judging it to be without consciousness." (Cf. also the corrupt B 42.)

Although there are only two clear examples the construction seems acceptable, since the Mohist logicians are compelled to express more complex relationships than other Chinese thinkers. The dropping of <u>chih</u> is not unknown elsewhere (cf. <u>Han Fei tzu</u>, Ch'en 612/2 人主於説也 皆如燕王學道也 "Rulers when it comes to taking advice are all like the King of Yen learning the Way").

The directive unit occupies the last nominal position in the sentence, a rule of word-order observed with the usual grammatical rigour of the dialectical chapters. It is a rule with one exception; when the main verb is <u>wu</u> 無   followed by <u>so</u> 所   (there is no example of <u>yu</u> 有   ) it is necessary to detach the directive from the final verb and attach it to <u>wu</u>, and it is therefore transposed in front of <u>wu</u>:

B 22 鑒 者 之 *臭 於 鑒 無 所 不 鑒

"What is lustrous (?) in the man looking at himself is mirrored in the mirror without exception" (cf. also A 65).

The directive unit may like other units be exposed, but for the sake of a contrast significant to the understanding of the sentence. In the single example in the Canons and Explanations, already discussed (p. 127), it heads the sentence and is resumed by yen, in the three examples in the Ta-ch'ü it precedes erh in a preliminary clause (p. 126).

Yeh 也

Since in most texts it is difficult to come to grips with the particle yeh it deserves close attention in a document in which words are never used casually. The units which it concludes are of two main types:

Type 1: the sentence pattern "(X) Y yeh" ("X is Y")

Type 2: the nominalised verbal or directive phrase in the form "X chih Y yeh" (B 77 不(知學之無益也) "not know that learning is useless", B 44 若(酒之於人也) "Like the effect of wine on a man"). X is a nominal unit subordinated to the verb, not necessarily its subject (Ta-ch'ü EC 2 (昔者之愛人也)非(今之愛人也) "Yesterday's love of men is not today's love of men", (愛臧之愛人也)乃(愛獲之愛人也) "The love of man which is love of Jack is the love of man which is love of Jill"). When subject "X chih" may be replaced by ch'i 其 . Chih itself is replaced by ch'i when X is a contrasted demonstrative subject (cf p. 76).

The reference of the nominalised verbal "X chih Y" phrase is to the action and not, as in the subjectless phrase nominalised by che 者 , to the agent. (A 98 彼舉(然者)以為(此其然也) "He refers to what is so and deems that it is so of the thing here", B 70

(若白者) 必白.... 故智 (其白也)　"What is like the white

is necessarily white.... Therefore I know it is white".) Exceptions, how-

ever, are found where ch'i stands in the place of "X chih" (A 26

(其害也) 非是也　"The one of them which is harmful is not this one".

Cf. B 52.)

The "X chih Y" phrase is generally although not invariably followed by

yeh, wherever it stands in the sentence.

B 57 (楹之搏也), 見之, (其於意也) 不易.

"In the case of a pillar being round, when we see it, its relation to the

idea does not substitute a new idea."

A 20　以 (其敢於是也) 命之

"One gives him the name ("Brave") because of what he does dare...."

B 65　(一法者之相與也) 盡, 若 (方之相合也)

"The agreement of things which have one standard is complete, like the

coincidence of squares."

Apart from this type of phrase, what kinds of element are marked off by

yeh at the beginning of the sentence? There appear to be no convincing

examples of other types of verbal unit, whether nominalised or not. We

do find nominal units, but confined to the following two types:

Type 3: a temporal word or proper name followed by a contrastive yeh.

The contrastive yeh is frequent after chin 今 "now", ch'ien 前　"be-

fore", shih 始 "in the beginning": B 32 (前也) 不懼, (今也)
懼 "Previously he was not afraid, now on the contrary he is

afraid." There is one instance with a proper name (a usage familiar in

the Analects):

Ta-ch'ü EC 4 藉(藏也)死而天下害, (吾特養

臧也)萬倍

"Supposing that if of all men Jack were to die the world would be harmed,

my special care for Jack would be ten-thousand-fold."

Type 4: A subject to which shih "the said" is adjunct is always followed

by yeh: A 78 (是名也)止於是實也 "The said name is

confined to the said object". B 53 (是聲也)(生)於今, 所義之

實處於古 "This vocal sound is born in the present, the object

taken as example resides in the past."

Ta-ch'ü NO 1 尚(是石也)白 "If the said stone is white"

(是石也)唯(=雖)大 "Although the said stone is big"

NO 3 (是璜也)是玉也 "This half-disc is this jade"

The purpose of this usage, also found in such texts as Chuang-tzu and

Hsün-tzu, is presumably to avoid confusion with a resumptive shih at the

beginning of the sentence.

Returning to type 1, since the Mohist logicians are especially concerned

with X being or not being Y the "(X) Y yeh" pattern appears in a variety

of guises. It is frequently embedded in verbal phrases, sometimes following verbs after which one would not normally expect it:

Ta-ch'ü EC 7　以臧為(其親也)而利之

"Benefiting Jack on the supposition that he is one's parent." (Contrast

the immediately following 以樂為利其子而為其子

欲之 "Desiring music for one's son on the supposition that it will

benefit him.")

B 53　舉(友富商也),是以名視(=示)人也.
指(是羹也),是以實視人也.

"Mentioning a friend as being a rich merchant is showing to others by

means of names. Pointing something out as being soup is showing to

others by means of the object."

A 39　二人而俱見(是楹也)

"They are two men and both see that it is a pillar."

B 8　狗假(鶴也),猶氏鶴也.

"'Loan-naming' a dog as being a crane is like using 'Crane' as a sur-

name."

This usage is important for the understanding of certain difficult sen-

tences in the Ta-ch'ü, in which we mark crucial phrases by letters:

No 3 　意[A]楹非意木也,意是楹之木也.
意[B](指之人也)非意人也,意[C](獲也)乃意禽也

"Visualising a pillar is not visualising wood, it is visualising the wood of

the said pillar. Visualising a finger as being the man is not visualising a

man; but visualising as being game on the contrary is visualising birds."

132

No 7 ^D(指之人也)與(首之人也)異，^E人之體 非 一 貌者也.

"The finger which is the man is different from the head which is the man, because the man's members are not things identical in appearance."

Cf. B 53 ^F(堯之義也) 生於今而處於古而異時

"Yao's being an example originates in the present yet he resides in the past and they are different times."

We cannot take B or D as "the finger's man" or F as "Yao's example" because when followed by yeh "X chih Y" is always a nominalised verbal phrase (cf. F, where yeh is absent). We cannot take D as "pointing out this man" or C as "visualising the game" because only units of types 2, 3, 4 can have a concluding yeh at the beginning of the sentence (cf. A, where yeh is absent). The strictness with which this rule applies to the "(X) Y yeh" sentence can be easily confirmed by running through the long sequences of such sentences in the Ta-ch'ü and Hsiao-ch'ü.

We find the "X Y yeh" pattern also in front of the conjunction erh 而 :

A 3, 4 「知」也者,(所以知也),而必知....

「慮」也者,(以其知有求也),而不必得之.

"In the case of the 'intelligence' it is the means by which one knows, and one knows with certainty..... In the case of 'thinking' it is to seek something by means of one's intelligence, but one does not necessarily find it."

When X and Y are nominal units the logical relationship is of identity or class membership. There is of course no counterpart to the Indo-European use of the copula before predicative adjectives, since words translatable as adjectives operate verbally and do not occupy the Y position of this pattern (Ta-ch'ü NO 1 苟（是石也）白 "If this stone is white"). We may class the pattern with nominal X and Y as type 1A, and distinguish from it type 1B, in which X and Y are verbal units, which may be single words or lengthy clauses.

In this sub-class no chih is added to the subject to nominalise the phrase, and the logical relationship between X and Y is much loosened. The nearest English equivalent of yeh in this construction is perhaps the unstressed "it's that" of the spoken language, used much more freely than the standard "It is that":

B 43 火鑠金，火多也．金靡炭，金多也．

"When the fire melts the metal it's that there's more fire, when the metal uses up the charcoal it's that there's more metal."

Here Y indicates the cause, and it is convenient to translate by "it is because....". In the sections on optics and mechanics, where yeh is infrequent, it is generally the marker of an explanatory following a descriptive clause:

B 25 加重於其一旁必捶，權重相若也．
.....摽必下，標得權也．

"If you lay a weight on one of the sides it is certain to decline, because they are equal in weight and leverage....... The tip is certain to fall, because it has gained in leverage."

Shih 是 intervening between X and Y is found only in type 1B. It generally preserves the strict relationship of identity or class member-ship; if there is loosening, it is in the direction of allowing Y to be an implication of X (not its cause or its grounds):

B 71 ˣ之 ˣ人之言可, 是不誖, 則是有可也

"If this man's statement is allowable, that is to say not erroneous, this implies that he allows something."

"X shih Y yeh" is used very freely, sometimes closely linking very short phrases (in the first example in the sentence above, which however lacks the yeh, the "shih Y" is even parenthetical):

A 66 異處不相盈. 相非是相外也.

"Different places do not fill each other. Not being each other is excluding each other."

B 77 是使智學之無益也, 是教也

"This is causing to know that learning is useless, which is teaching."

There remain many "Y yeh" sentences in which we cannot identify the preceding clause or sequence of clauses as X. Before considering them we must exclude cases of final yeh which belong to other types. Those of type 2 ("X chih Y yeh" at the end of the sentence) are easily identified.

There are also uses of single words often associated with a final <u>yeh</u>, which we may group under a type 5:

Type 5A: <u>Yeh</u> after a passive verb following <u>k'o</u> 可 (A 75 牆外之利害(未可知也) "Whether it is beneficial or harmful outside the wall is not yet knowable"). This usage with <u>k'o</u> (and also with <u>tsu</u> 足) is common to most pre-Han texts.

Type 5B: <u>Yeh</u> after "<u>wei</u> 謂 X", where the object X indicates what is referred to, not what is said (cf. p. 117).

There remains a further sub-class of type 1:

Type 1C: The affirmation or denial of one alternative, expressed by <u>yeh</u> at the end of a verbal sentence or <u>fei</u> 非 in stead of <u>pu</u> 不 in front of the verb. In general we may say that a verbal sentence answers a "What?" question and allows any number of answers, and that the addition of <u>yeh</u> makes it the answer to a "Yes or no?" question, although it may not always be significant to analyse the limited number of possibilities involved into distinct pairs. Most Chinese thinkers use this form so freely that one gets into the habit of assuming that any final <u>yeh</u> can be put in this sub-class and then ignored. But the later Mohists use it much more rarely and with discrimination, in contexts where the alternatives envisaged are generally plain.

B 3 有*之實也而後謂之, 無之實也則無謂也.
不 若*殹(?)與美. 謂是 則 是因美也, 謂也(=他)
則 是非美, 無 謂則*假也.

(Implicit questions: Q 1 "Is there this object or not?", Q 2 "If not, is there a reference to this object or not?")

"Only when (A 1 is that) there is this object does one refer to it; if (A 1 is that) there is not (A 2 is that) there is not the reference.

(Q 3 "Is this object the beautiful one or not?")

It is not like 'mansion' (?) and 'beautiful'. If the reference is to this one, of course (A 3 is that) this is the beautiful one; if the reference is to another one, it is not that this is the beautiful one; and if it does not have the reference (A 3 is that) the reverse applies."

B 35 所謂非同也,則異也. 同則或謂之「狗」,其或謂之「犬」也,異則或謂之「牛」,其或謂之「馬」也,俱無勝,是不辯也.辯也者,或謂之是,或謂之非,當者勝也.

(Implicit questions: Q 1 "Is the debate over one object?", Q 2 "In either case, is it over one name?")

" If it is not that they are talking about the same thing it is that they are talking about different things (A 1). Should it be that when talking about the same thing one man calls it 'whelp' and the other 'dog' (A 2 when A 1 is 'Yes'), or that when talking about different things one man calls it 'ox' and the other 'horse' (A 2 when A 1 is 'No'), so that neither wins, this is failing to dispute over alternatives. In the case of 'disputation over alternatives' it is that one calls it 'this' and the other 'not this', and the one who fits the fact wins (A 1, 2)."

In this case it will be seen that the shih resumes a long sequence of

137

clauses, in which each of the first pair ends in yeh. The effect is to render them hypothetical; we therefore translate by "should it be that...".
The fact that an added yeh does not stop a clause being hypothetical as well as the closeness with which shih can link with a preceding clause (already illustrated, p. 135), are relevant to the analysis of the next two examples. Both are at first sight difficult to untangle, but fortunately are identical in structure. The crucial clause in each ends in yeh and intervenes between tse and shih; and in each it answers in the negative an implicit question raised by the clause preceding tse:

A 75 厲外之利害(未可知也),趨之而得 *力,
則弗趨也,是以所疑止所欲也

(Q. Do you go after it or not?)

"If whether it is beneficial or harmful beyond the wall is not yet knowable, but if you go after it you will get the coin, then should it be that you do not go after it, this is checking desire on account of doubt."

B 38 子智是,有(=又)智是吾所先舉重,
則子智是而不智吾所先舉也,
是一謂有智焉,有不智焉也.

(Q. Do you know the thing that I mentioned previously or not?)

"If you know the said thing, and know too that it is the 'double' of the thing I mentioned previously (i.e. that some objects are called by both names, A 86), then should it be that while knowing the said thing you do not know the thing I mentioned previously, then this is knowing some but not knowing others among objects called by one name."

138

Finding list

CH'EN Ch'i-yu 陳奇猷 , <u>Han Fei tzǔ chi-shih</u> 韓非子集釋

                 Peking 1958.

CHOU Fa-kao 周法高 , <u>Chung-kuo ku-dai yü-fa</u> 中國古代語法

                 Taipei, 1959-

HSÜ Wei-yü 許維遹, <u>Lü-shih ch'un-ch'iu chi-shih</u> 呂氏春秋集釋

                 Peking 1955.

LIU Wen-tien 劉文典 , <u>Chuang-tzǔ pu-cheng</u> 莊子補正

                 Commercial Press, 1947.

PI Yüan 畢沅 , <u>Mo-tzǔ</u> 墨子 (<u>Ssǔ-pu pei-yao</u> 四部備要)

PULLEYBLANK, E.G. <u>Fei</u> 非   <u>wei</u> 唯   <u>and certain related words</u>

                 (Studia serica Bernhard Karlgren dedicata,

                 1959)

<u>Shih chi</u> 史記 , Chung-hua Book Company, Peking 1959.

SUN Yi-jang 孫詒讓, <u>Mo-tzǔ chien-ku</u> 墨子閒詁 , Peking 1954.

T'AN Chieh-fu 譚戒甫 , <u>Mo-pien fa-wei</u> 墨辯發微 , Pe-

                 king 1958.

TS'EN Chung-mien 岑仲勉 , <u>Mo-tzǔ ch'eng-shou ko-p'ien chien-chu</u>

                 墨子城守各篇簡注 , Peking

                 1958.

WU Yü-chiang 吳毓江, <u>Mo-tzǔ chiao-chu</u> 墨子校注   <u>Tu-li</u>

                 <u>ch'u-pan she</u> 獨立出版社, 1944.

Note 1: The dialectical chapters are most conveniently studied in the edition of T'an Chieh-fu. The present study often differs from T'an both in its interpretations and in the division and numbering of the Canons and of the Ta-ch'ü fragments; unfortunately it is impossible to justify the divergences within the limits of this article. The Harvard-Yenching concordance to Mo-tzŭ is an indispensible tool for the study of the language, although its punctuation is very erratic and it incorporates the emendations of Sun Yi-jang in the text (the supposed variants at the bottom of the page are often the original readings of the standard edition, that of the Taoist Patrology). Ta-ch'ü and Hsiao-ch'ü references follow the rearrangement in my Later Mohist treatises on ethics and logic reconstructed from the Ta-ch'ü (forthcoming Asia Major)

Note 2: Several instances of yeh 也 and nearly every instance of wen 文 are generally recognised to be corruptions of chih 之 . It is remarkable that in the former cases chih is always the particle, in the latter always the pronoun.

Note 3: Chü "lift" appears without the radical in A 21 and one of the instances in B 5. The Japanese Hōryaku 寳 曆 edition also omits it in the other instance in B 5. But all editions have the radical in the remaining example, B 10.

Note 4: Kung-sun Lung's Essay on Meanings and Things Journal of

Oriental Studies 2/2 ('1955)

Note 5: Cf. Pulleyblank op. cit.

Note 6: Chuang tzu ch. 17 (Liu 6 下, 25B)

Note 7: Logic of the Mohist Hsiao-ch'ü, Toung Pao 51/1 ('64) 10

DISCUSSION ON GRAHAM'S PAPER: THE GRAMMAR OF THE MOHIST DIALECTICAL CHAPTERS

Malmqvist: In this text the author takes very great pains in defining terms. I have found the same thing in the Kung-yang and the Ku-liang. There is one example which goes like this: 求之為言得不得未可知之辭也 "the meaning of ch'iu is that whether you obtain it or not you don't know".

Graham: Yes, they are great definers. They also have lists of words with several meanings.

Egerod: I find it interesting on the first page by a well-known grammarian to see that the text under discussion is unique in the history of classical Chinese and it shows up the logical structure of the language, but does it also show up the linguistic structure of the language? I think you have argued very well that it is a linguistic structure that has been used with such force for logical means. But reading some of these sentences one asks, have they done this by using ordinary Chinese or is this some kind of a special formular language that does not fit the ordinary build-up. I don't know what your own immediate impression is. Is everything here good language and is it just that it is more consistent with logic, or have they also made innovations for their own logical purposes?

Graham: Yes, I think they have made innovations. It must have seemed to be an extraordinarily Chinese. On the other hand I think there is an interest in seeing how they did it. I mean it is interesting to see how they said "X is not not Y" in Ancient Chinese.

Egerod: The last thing you expect the structure of a language to be is logical.

Graham: Yes, but I didn't mean that the logical structure is the same thing as the linguistic structure, it is just one aspect of it.

Egerod: Yes, of course, One feels tempted to ask to what extent are they then influenced by the structure of the language in this specific kind of logical structure. You make the statement that they "were concerned with logical precision, to which grammatical precision is an essential means". And since they must work within the grammar of the language it sounds as if their logic may then to a certain extent be influenced by that grammar they do have available. I don't know whether you think so or not.

Graham: Yes, I feel so. I think it is interesting the way they handle the demonstratives. It must reflect the use of the language.

Kratochvil: You speak of a rapidly developing language which is reflected in the fact that every text is to some extent peculiar in grammar as well as in vocabulary. It seems to me the this has certain implications which I am not at all clear about. Would it mean that a language, in this case Chinese, is developing more rapidly at some times than others, and that the peculiarity of grammar and vocabulary of texts coming from a particular period is necessarily a reflection of rapid development in that period? What does, in fact, rapid development of language mean?

Graham: I agree that the variety in itself is not a proof of a rapid development. In a general way I think one has the right to say that this was a time in the Chinese culture when people were forced to think and say things which they hadn't thought about before. Of course they sometime had to say things which hadn't been sayable before.

Egerod: There is the opposite point to it also, I guess, that part of the reason for the existence of philosophy is the very fact that language does not develop fast enough. The culture sort of changes faster and some of the contents of usual words do not longer seem applicable, so they have to talk about it. I mean part of philosophy is always the fact that language is slower than philosophy. It seems to me that these philosophers are sailing pretty close to the wind, I mean they are keeping to the grammar that is given and that must have some influence on what they are doing. I don't suggest that they cannot think beyond it. You talk about "the manner in which particles serve only the logical structure of the sentence". I mean we are in the middle of something where we almost equate the logic with the way the grammar works, which I am sure is very significant

Graham: I am not suggesting that this applies anywhere else of course.

Egerod: It is remarkable to see that they graphically distinguished pronouns and particles commonly written with the same character. Do you think that this has been done in any other text?

Graham: It is the only one known to me.

Egerod: At least it all seems to show that we do not have one more dialect but a more conscious attempt at being oneself. It would not fit into the pattern of Karlgren's excursions where all he would have said is that this is a different dialect, and by no tricks that he uses would your interpretation have come out. It must be consciously done because of the remarkably consistent way it has been applied.

Again it is very nice to see that you do negate "fei" with "pu". What we have been treating as nominal is treated as if it were not. Just as you treat "wei" in itself as being verbal by means of "pu". Then whatever "fei" is, whether it logically contains the "pu" already or not, it gets negated by "pu". So one of the main criteria for making a distinction disappears in the air. I think that is a very neat trick.

Egerod: I like the incredible strictness of this text even down to the point that all the "pu" and the "wu" go just along with the pattern you want them to. Also the clear contrast between "fei niu" and "fei niu yeh". If there should be people around who still think that "yeh" is nothing but "ultimate emphasis" I think this will disprove it for ever. Is there a difference between "fei niu" and a similar construction with or without "che"?

Graham: I don't think there is a case with "fei" and "che".

Egerod: It is interesting how in many cases the absence of "yeh" functions very much like the presence of "che".

Alexis Rygaloff

LE SYNTAGME NOMINAL COMPLEXE, LA FONCTION DE <u>DE</u> 的 ET LES VALEURS DE <u>YOU</u> 有

Le terme de syntagme nominal complexe sert ici à regrouper tout l'ensemble des situations où la détermination d'un nom est effectuée par d'autres éléments que ceux auxquels on a l'habitude de recourir pour définir la classe nominale en chinois moderne - comme yī-běn ou zhèi-<u>běn</u> dans <u>yī-běn shū</u> "un livre" ou zhèi-běn shū "ce livre-ci" - et qui eux-mêmes ne sauraient se définir autrement que dans le cadre d'une entité - conventionnellement, l'"adjectif déterminatif" - dont la raison d'être est d'assurer un premier degré de détermination du nom.

Les types à considérer pourront donc être représentés par des exemples comme ceux-ci:

1. D'une part, <u>wǒ-de shū</u> "mes (mon) livres", <u>xuésheng-de péngyou</u> "les (l', des, un) amis des (de l') étudiants", <u>zhèi-ge xuésheng-de yī-ge péngyou</u> "un ami de cet étudiant" etc..., où le déterminant est lui-même nominal.

2. D'autre part, <u>mǎi shū de xuésheng</u> "les (l') étudiants qui achètent des (un) livres", <u>xuésheng mǎi de shu</u> "les (le) livres que les (l') étudiants achètent" etc..., où le déterminant est constitué par ou autour d'un verbe.

On ne saurait évidemment s'arrêter au fait que dans un cas comme dans l'autre les éléments de la détermination ne sont pas seulement disposés conformément à la règle de position, mais qu'ils sont de plus démarqués par la particule <u>de</u>; qu'ils le sont au moins facultativement, comme dans les cas qui évoquent la "possession inaliénable", lorsque le déterminé est représenté par la désignation d'une partie du corps ou un terme de proximité, et le déterminant par un pronom personnel singulier - p. ex. <u>wǒ(-de) shǒu</u> "ma main", <u>nǐ(-de) fùqin</u> "ton père" - alors que <u>de</u> est impossible dans le syntagme simple, régi exclusivement par la règle de position: il ne peut suffire, en effet, de définir <u>de</u> comme une marque **du** syntagme nominal complexe, introduite par une règle de portée moindre et dont le jeu est subordonné à l'application de celle-ci.

Il va sans dire qu'au moins dans les cas où le déterminant est verbal (exemples 2 ci-dessus), le syntagme est le résultat d'une transformation, qu'il est obtenu à partir d'un énoncé complet. Dès lors il importe d'abord de rechercher chaque fois la forme de la phrase sous-jacente, puis de rendre explicites les règles de transformation qui permettent d'aboutir au syntagme en partant de la phrase supposée.

a) xuésheng mǎi de shū

b) mǎi shū de xuésheng

Sans doute, en dernière analyse, les deux syntagmes dérivent-ils d'une seule et même phrase:

c) xuésheng mǎi shū "les (l') étudiants achètent des (un) livres".

Mais pour obtenir une dérivation directe dans les deux cas, il faudrait qu'en tout état de cause la règle soit complexe, ou si l'on préfère qu'il y ait deux règles distinctes, puisque tantôt il y a permutation des éléments et non seulement introduction de de, et tantôt non.

En fait, au moins dans l'un des deux cas, la dérivation est certainement indirecte. Elle ne saurait être effectuée directement sans laisser inexpliqué le fait que s'efface, en passant de la phrase unique aux deux syntagmes, la différence de contenu qui, au départ, sépare les deux éléments nominaux: du fait de la position, xuésheng, dans (c) est en effet défini, et shū indéfini.

La façon la plus simple d'effacer cette différence avant d'arriver au syntagme est sans doute de faire dériver (a) non directement de (c), mais d'une transformation préalable de cette phrase, obtenue en jouant uniquement des faits de position:

d) shū, xuésheng mǎi, où l'élément représenté par shū, même s'il n'est pas nécessairement défini, peut, comme xuésheng, avoir cette valeur: "les (le) livres, les (l') étudiants les (l', en) achètent".

La règle de dérivation recherchée s'appliquerait donc à deux phrases différentes, l'une étant une dérivation de l'autre; mais en revanche cette règle serait simple (unique) puisque dans les deux cas il y a permutation, et non seulement introduction de de.

En réalité, avec cette solution, la difficulté n'a été que déplacée: en partant de (c) et (d) pour aboutir respectivement à (b) et (a) on supprime bien la différence qui fait problème, mais on la supprime à l'envers. Ce qui pose un problème maintenant c'est le changement de contenu qui accompagne dans les deux cas le passage de la phrase au syntagme: le fait

qu'on passe dans un cas comme dans l'autre d'un énoncé portant sur un
ensemble d'individus conçu comme une totalité - à la limite d'un individu
constituant cet ensemble à lui seul - à une situation où une partie du
même ensemble est nécessairement encore qu'implicitement exclue -
étant, là encore, exclus à la limite tous les individus qui la composent
sauf un seul. La forme obtenue à l'arrivée (le syntagme) définit en
quelque sorte une "moitié" à l'intérieur de l'ensemble visé par la base
(xuésheng ou shū); elle implique une bipartition de cet ensemble en ex-
cluant l'autre "moitié": parmi les étudiants, ceux qui achètent des livres
à l'exclusion de ceux qui n'en achètent pas; ou parmi les livres, ceux qui

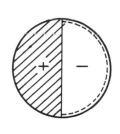

sont achetés par les étudiants par opposition aux
livres que ceux-ci n'achètent pas (fig. 1). Il faut
donc qu'au départ, dans l'énoncé sous-jacent qui
donne la raison de cette bipartition, celle-ci soit
si l'on peut dire prévue. Or, celle-ci n'est prévue
que dans la mesure où ce qui est visé n'est pas la
totalité, mais seulement une partie quelconque d'un
ensemble donné, autrement dit, si le nom qui se
trouvera à la base du syntagme possède d'avance,
dans la phrase sous-jacente, un contenu indéfini

fig 1

(fig. 2). Il faut remarquer que le chinois ignore
cette ambiguité bien connue qui n'est levée en français (ou ailleurs) qu'au
moyen d'une virgule: (b) ne s'interprète en aucun cas comme "les étudiants, qui achètent des livres", mais uniquement comme "les étudiants

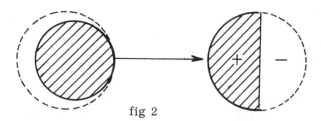

fig 2

qui achètent des livres", autrement dit, "ceux des étudiants qui ..." im-
pliquant que tous ne sont pas dans ce cas; il s'agit donc toujours de la
situation où c'est l'article indéfini que fait intervenir le français dans la
phrase sous-jacente: "un - ou des - étudiant ...". En fait, s'il s'agissait
seulement de rendre compte de (a), il serait certainement préférable de
s'en tenir à (c) xuésheng mǎi shu, où le contenu de shū est bien indéfini.
Mais (b) est également en cause, et on sait qu'il est impossible, en
jouant uniquement sur la position, de transformer cette phrase de manière
à obtenir le même effet pour xuésheng.

La seule transformation de (c) qui ait pour effet de modifier le contenu de
xuésheng dans le sens voulu, et qui a l'avantage de s'appliquer aussi bien

à (d) pour ce qui est de shū, consiste à introduire le nom qui figure en tête de l'énoncé à l'aide de yŏu "y avoir", étant entendu que de ce fait la phrase devient complexe:

c') yŏu xuésheng măi shū "il y a des étudiants qui achètent des livres" résulte de l'imbrication de deûx phrases élémentaires, yŏu xuésheng et xuésheng măi shū; et de même;

d') yŏu shū xuésheng măi "il y a des livres que les étudiants achètent", les phrases élémentaires étant alors yŏu shū et shū xuésheng măi.

Ainsi, aucun des deux syntagmes ne serait obtenu par dérivation directe à partir de la phrase primaire (c): l'énoncé sous-jacent, complexe dans les deux cas, serait de toute façon le produit d'une transformation, celle-ci s'exerçant dans l'un des deux cas - (d) → (a) - sur une phrase encore simple, mais déjà transformée. Et la règle, toujours unique, qui conduit au syntagme, fait maintenant apparaître la particule de non plus comme une forme primaire, mais comme une dérivation (une "réécriture") - de yŏu - "il y en a qui"→"ceux qui" - dont la fonction est d'accompagner la permutation des élément de la phrase sous-jacente pour transformer celle-ci en syntagme. En partant de la forme ⌜yŏu N + X⌝ la règle de dérivation s'énonce en effet comme ceci: déplacer X (le reste de la phrase) en tête, et remplacer yŏu par de.

Il est clair que la particule de reste en relation avec yŏu dans les cas où la détermination est effectuée par un nom (exemples 1 ci-dessus): xuésheng-de shū ne saurait s'interpréter autrement qu'à partir de xuésheng yŏu shū "les (l') étudiants ont des (un) livres". Mais il peut sembler à première vue qu'il s'agisse alors d'une situation toute différente: yŏu, verbe unique d'une phrase simple, met en rapport deux élément nominaux qui, dans le syntagme, conservent leurs positions respectives, la dérivation étant assurée uniquement par la substitution de de à yŏu. Il pourrait y avoir, en effet, une distinction à faire pour de, qui s'expliquerait assez par celle que l'on admet pour yŏu:"avoir" et "y avoir". Et cependant zhèr-de shū "les livres qui sont ici" dérive de zhèr yŏu shū, où yŏu a bien la seconde valeur, tout comme wŏ-de shū de wŏ yŏu shū.

A la vérité, il n'est nullement certain que cette double valeur de yŏu soit beaucoup plus qu'un effet de traduction. Ce qui, ici, impose une distinction ce n'est pas seulement qu'en français, par exemple, yŏu se traduit tantôt par "avoir" et tantôt par "y avoir" - ou en anglais par "have" et "there is" - c'est aussi que la statistique porte à considérer d'abord la première de ces équivalences. Or, il est assez évident qu'en partant de wŏ yŏu shū traduit par "j'ai des livres" on ne passe pas sans discontinuité à zhèr yŏu shū "ici il y a des livres". Mais l'inverse n'est pas vrai: rien ne s'oppose à ce que soit conservée dans wǒ yǒu shū la valeur que prend yǒu dans zhèr yǒu shū – "quant à moi, il y a des livres" - et que soit du même coup reconnue en chinois pour l'expression de la possession une situation analogue à celle qui prévaut dans de très nombreuses langues, comme le russe, le turc, le mongol, le japonais ... Mais alors il devient impossible de considérer comme le "sujet" de la phrase l'élément représenté par wǒ: wǒ, tout comme zhèr, n'apparaît plus que comme un complément circonstanciel, et c'est shū qui devient le sujet. Quant à yǒu c'est, dès lors, et pour tous ses emplois, aux verbes intransitifs qu'il conviendrait de le rattacher, ces verbes ayant, comme chacun sait, la propriété d'admettre le sujet aussi bien avant qu'après: et en effet, yǒu shū "il y a des livres" et shū, yǒu "des livres, il y en a", sont des énoncés également acceptables, tout comme lái kèren "il vient des visiteurs" et kèren lái "les invités viennent".

Le passage se fait donc sans discontinuité de zhèr yǒu shū à wǒ yǒu shū; et de même, il n'y a aucune raison pour attribuer à yǒu une valeur différente dans le type de phrase dont on a reconnu que le syntagme nominal complexe était une transformation directe: yǒu shū xuésheng mǎi ou yǒu xuésheng mǎi shū; car il importe peu à cet égard qu'il y ait une différence de complexité au niveau de la phrase, et pas davantage que dans l'un des deux cas la phrase comporte un complément circonstanciel et non dans l'autre. S'agissant du second point, rien ne s'oppose à ce que celui-ci soit supprimé dans la phrase simple - yǒu shū -, ni, à l'inverse, qu'à la phrase complexe un circonstanciel soit ajouté: par exemple, zuótian yǒu shū xuésheng mǎi "hier il y avait des livres que les étudiant achetaient".

L'intérêt du dernier énoncé pour le problème qui nous occupe à présent est de faire apparaître le complément circonstanciel comme un troisième élément de la phrase sous-jacente. Sans doute, cet élément n'est-il pas nécessairement autonome, dans la mesure où il peut également figurer avant le verbe principal (mǎi), et se retrouver dans la même position après la transformation en syntagme, comme une partie du déterminant: xuésheng zuótian mǎi-de shū. Mais ce qu'il importe de remarquer, c'est qu'il conserve sa position en tout état de cause, même lorsque dans la phrase sous-jacente il figure en tête, avant yǒu, et que dans la transformation en syntagme il a un comportement propre: zuótian yǒu shū xuésheng mǎi → zuótian xuésheng mǎi-de shū. En effet, le modèle de la phrase sous-jacente devenant [C] + yǒu N + X, la règle consiste à transporter X devant yǒu remplacé par de, la position du (ou des) complément circonstanciel demeurant inchangée.

Et il apparaît en même temps que la détermination nominale effectuée par un nom - zhèr-de shū comme wǒ-de shū - ne représente qu'un cas particulier de la même règle, où X est vide et C nécessairement présent.

DISCUSSION ON RYGALOFF'S PAPER: LE SYNTAGME NOMINAL

COMPLEXE, LA FONCTION DE DE 的 ET LES VALEURS DE YǑU 有 .

Malmqvist: In the sentence "shū, xuésheng mǎi", do you mean that "shū" has a definite reference.

Rygaloff: Yes, or at least it may have. What I mean is that in the sentence "xuésheng mǎi shū", "shū" cannot have a definite reference, but in "shū, xuésheng mǎi", "shū" may have a definite reference.

Egerod: But not necessarily.

Malmqvist: I would like to say that "shū, xuésheng mǎi", is really a bound form occurring in sentences like "shū, xuésheng mǎi, kěshi máobǐ bù mǎi".

Rygaloff: It you want to translate into Chinese: "the books, the students buy them", you would have to say this.

Egerod: Doesn't it rather mean: "des livres, les étudiants en achetent".

Rygaloff: Yes, of course, it may mean that also: it is a question of context.

Malmqvist: If I heard the sentence "yǒu shū xuésheng mǎi" I would immediately interpret it as "yǒu shū de hùa xuésheng mǎi", "if there are books students will buy them".

Rygaloff: How would you say: "there are books which the students buy".

Malmqvist: "yǒu de shū xuésheng mǎi".

Rygaloff: I think you could say both.

Malmqvist: Could you negate it, "méi yǒu shū xuésheng mǎi".

Rygaloff: Yes, of course.

Chang: You cannot say that, it must be: "méi yǒu shū xuésheng pù mǎi".

Rygaloff: I don't think it matters so much. I am of the opinion that an underlying sentence may sound unusual.

Malmqvist: Then you can equally well argue that the underlying form for "yī ben shu" is "yī běn de shū". It isn't used but..

Rygaloff: Well, the thing I wanted to say is that at least these cases imply a derivation from a whole sentence. There are no underlying sentences in the case of the "syntagma".

Malmqvist: I cannot see that your arguments will be in any way weakened if you accepted as underlying forms "yǒu de shū xuésheng mǎi" and "yǒu de xuésheng mǎi shū".

Rygaloff: I accept it very well. But you have to get to that first.

Kratochvil: I would like to question that there must be the same kernel sentence for both "xuésheng mǎi de shū" and "mǎi shū de xuésheng".

Rygaloff: Could you find another one?

Kratochvil: I can't really find another one, but it is possible to imagine that, taking the latter sentence "mǎi shū de xuésheng" for example, it could be imbedded in another sentence. The kernel sentence would then be "xuésheng [verb]" rather than "xuésheng mǎi shū", and the two sentences would not be derived from the same kernel sentence.

Egerod: I don't think you have any reason to think that if you have some underlying sentence about "xuésheng mǎi shū" that the "shū" in the underlying sentence has anything to do with the "shū" in the derived sentence, nor do I think that the "xuésheng" in your underlying sentence is the "xuésheng" in the derived sentence. What you have is "xuésheng mǎi". By means of this "de" what you say is that this thing you want to enter into another sentence. In the other sentence there happens to be a "shū" which belongs in the other sentence. It does not belong in this sentence. You just transfer the potential object, which you don't know what is. You nominalize that the way you do with "suǒ" in the classical language. You just say that this "xuésheng mǎi" might have an object. We do not know what it is but we nominalize it and enter it into another sentence, where it then becomes evident that it is being used as an adjective to "shū" in another sentence. But that "shū" has nothing to do with your kernel sentence "shū", because in your kernel sentence there is no object. You do not know what it is. The same thing when you say "mǎi shū de xuésheng". You don't know the "xuésheng". Exactly what is interesting about this kernel sentence is that there is no subject, and what you say is that there might be a subject. This potential subject we nominalize and then put it into another sentence, because you have to have two sentences and the "xuésheng" is part of another sentence and the "shū" is part of another sentence.

Rygaloff: No, I don't think so. I think that your part is the part of the heare Of course, the hearer hears "xuésheng mǎi" and he does not know what comes next. But the speaker knows.

Egerod: It has nothing to do with whether he knows. It is whether it is the same sentence.

Rygaloff: I think it is. I can't analyze this sort of things except as being transformations of the same sentence.

Egerod: If you have a statement that says that "xuésheng" sells something, of course it is a sentence since there is an object. But now you have something else, you have two sentences. You have one sentence that says that there are some books and you know something about the books. The student are in the other sentence. You start as if you have only one sentence. But you don't. The interesting thing is that you operate with one sentence which has students and another sentence which has books. And you are putting two sentences together and it depends on what it is you don't know. In one case it is the object you don't know, in the other it is the subject you don't know and of course they come out differently whether it is the object that is in the other sentence or it is the subject. The speaker choses to make it from two different sentences, one without an object, one without a subject. Those books that you put into the kernel sentence are not in that one and those students are not the same students.

Rygaloff: No, I don't agree with that. What I agree with is that there are differences in sentences a and b, and they are differences which can very well be accounted for by the fact that there is a difference of function, one is the object and one is the subject, so there must be differences in the derived phrases as well.

Egerod: But it is not a derived sentence. It is a fusion of two sentences. You forget about the "shū hěn guì" or whatever it is they say about then. It is another sentence. Give us the whole sentence and then let us see exactly what the two sentences are that you have merged together.

Rygaloff: This is not the problem. These phrases can be used in all sorts of contexts. What I mean is that a complex phrase like this implies a complex sentence which is complete.

Egerod: It implies two underlying sentences.

Rygaloff: I made a distinction. I am not saying that they are the same.

Malmqvist: I think that the two translations of "yǒu", "have", and "there is" cannot be the sole reason why we think that the functions are different. I think one has to take into account the transformational potential of the forms. You can transform "zhèr yǒu shū" into "shū zài zhèr" but you cannot transform "xuésheng yǒu shū" into "shū zài zhèr". That seems to point to the fact that we are dealing with two forms of "yǒu" which have different weight and different potentials.

Rygaloff: I don't think it is a very strong argument because the point is that "xuésheng" in these cases is not marked and the possibility of making the transformations you just mentioned implies that one of the elements is marked. You cannot say "shū zài wǒ" but you can say "shū zài wǒ zhèr" and "wǒ zhèr yǒu shū". I think it is semantically more satisfactory to be able to stick to the same value in all cases.

Kratochvil: Did you try this out with other sentences involving some other lexical items.

Rygaloff: I don't think it is a very strong argument because the point is as I can see in all cases where "de" is involved you have the possibility of getting an underlying sentence with "yǒu". E.g. "tā lái de shíhou" - "yǒu shíhou tā lái".

Kratochvil: What about "Zhōngguó de dìtú".

Rygaloff: "Zhōngguó yǒu dìtú", "as far as China is concerned, there are maps", why not? The only place where it doesn't work is "tā lái de huà". I don't think "yǒu huà tā lái" is thinkable. This is the limit.

Egerod: I would like once again to make the point that I think that we can't say that "the books which I buy" is derived from "I buy books". It seems to me that this is what you are doing here. You are saying that "the students" or "students" "buy books". From this you derive "the books which the students buy". I am trying to make the point that these sentences are not directly related. What we have to relate is that "the books are expensive" or "books are expensive" and "the students buy", alright "books", but what happens with "books" whether is is "books" or "the books" has nothing to do with that sentence but with the other one, the one in which it is embedded.

Rygaloff: Yes, of course, with that I agree.

Egerod: But then I can't see that you can derive "mǎi shū de xuésheng" from "yǒu xuésheng mǎi shū". You must derive it from "shū hěn guì" or "shū zài zhèr" or something pulus "xuésheng mǎi" or xuésheng mǎi shū" with an object, but it is by having these two sentences that you get your problem of what happens. You don't have the problem if you only have the basic sentence, just as you don't have the problem if you only have "students buy books". You don't derive anything from that. And therefore your "books" belongs to that other sentence, just as your "students" belong to that other sentence, when you derived the two. It is very important to me to point out that you are putting both subject and object in the same original sentence when actually one of them belongs in another sentence. And it is that other sentence that influences your outcome.

Rygaloff: You mean the sentence in which the whole phrase is used?

Egerod: Yes.

Rygaloff: I agree with that. But a kernel sentence is not always transformed but transformable. When you analyze a sentence with a nominal phrase you have to consider the whole sentence, but for my purpose it was not needed. I think it is understood that these phrases don't exist by themselves. I am just considering the stage where these phrases which appear in a sentence have to be analyzed.

Egerod: Yes, but if you say that "the students buy books" and from this you derive "the books which the students buy", then that is not right because those books have nothing to do with that sentence.

Rygaloff: No, I am doing the opposite. I am not interested in transforming "the students buy books". I am interested in finding the underlying sentence of "xuésheng mǎi de shū" and "mǎi shū de xuésheng". This is what I am interested in.

Egerod: Yes, but there is not one underlying sentence. There are two underlying sentences.

Rygaloff: Yes, I agree. But what I say is this problem of the last analysis. I do not find the possibility of deriving both phrases from the same sentence directly. You don't even accept that?

Egerod: No, because I think that so much has to do with what happens to it in that other sentence. Why do you want to combine those two? It has to do with what happens with the common element in the two of them.

Rygaloff: There are many instances where a phrase like "xuésheng mǎi de shū" or "mǎi shū de xuésheng" can be used in the same context. Of course with the difference that the distribution of "shū" and "xuésheng" is not the same. At some stage you can very well consider both.

Egerod: I think you are comparing, not deriving.

Rygaloff: You have to accept that some sentences are kernels and some are derived, and personally I do accept it and for me a sentence like "xuésheng mǎi shū" is an elementary sentence from which many transformations can be made, but nothing can be expressed by "xuésheng mǎi de shū" without making it complete, and of course many things can be added into it.

Kratochvil: I can't really see that the sentence "xuésheng mǎi shū" is complete. What makes it complete? Is it an article of faith?

Rygaloff: No, it isn't. It is just that if you suppress any part of "xuésheng mǎi shū" it has to be supplied from the context.

Kratochvil: If I suggested that the sentence "mǎi shū" is complete what will be the argument against it?

Rygaloff: Well, it is a semantical element. Someone has to buy books.

Kratochvil: You could equally well say that "xuésheng mǎi shū" is incomplete because you don't know when.

Egerod: Is "yǒu shū" complete?

Rygaloff: Yes. I would say so.

Egerod: In a very few contexts perhaps, but in practical language it doesn't say much.

Rygaloff: I think that this problem of what is complete and what is incomplete maybe cannot be proved but can be supported by interrelations between questions and answers. What is a possible question to a possible answer and vice versa. These are things which you can consider.

Egerod: We have in your two examples here two different functions of "de", and one of them happens to remind us of classical Chinese "sǔo". I was glad about your pause because you have "sǔo" exactly there: "xuésheng sǔo mǎi de shū". In this case what "de" does is that it represents an unknown object which for some reason we also want to use in another sentence, because you want to say something about some books, whereas in "mǎi shū de"

what is missing according to your idea about a complete sentence is of course
the subject. In that case the "de" then tells us that we happen to have a subject for this "mǎi shū" and that is the thing which we are now going to combine with another sentence, and so we get this construction which you call
a). But as long as you say that from something that is in your idea a complete
sentence you derive something that is not then you have not told the whole
story, and I wanted to force you to tell the whole story because I felt it
then becomes clear that these two functions of "de" are very different,
and that they on formal grounds can be distinguished in the modern language.

Rygaloff: Yes, I agree. But I don't think it has anything to do with "de".It
is in fact that the function of the head in the underlying sentence is in one
case the object and in one case the subject, and there is of course a trace
of it which remains in the derived phrase. But I don't think it involves any
difference in the case of "de". The relation is the same. The differences
are accounted for in other considerations which are outside my problem.

Egerod: The only thing we can do is to count what do they have in common
and what they don't. They both make some sort of subordination so they
have that in common, but there are perhaps other things which they do not
have in common, so unless we make it specific what it is, we haven't told
the whole story. Whether we then say it is the same "de" or not really is
a trivial question, when we do not tell the whole story of the function.

Rygaloff: But in the case of "suǒ" there is also something else. You are
putting the emphasis on the deictic function of "suǒ", precisely the book
that I bought. Doesn't it also have the meaning of "all the books"?

Egerod: I don't care so much about that. But it is a very funny kind of
thing that occurs only in one sentence and not in the other.

Rygaloff: This is important for the interpretation of "suo" because the interesting point is that the effect of the use of "suǒ", semantically speaking,
is empty in most cases, "xuésheng mǎi de shū" and "xuésheng suǒ mai de
shū" is the same. The only case where it has a complete change of meaning
is in "suǒ yǒu". Concerning the difference of "yǒu", I consider there are
two elements in the meaning of "yǒu" and I think there is a very interesting
play of meaning in the two features. One of the features is the non-integralit
of the set in opposition to "shì" in "zhèr shì shū" and "zhèr yǒu shū". The
difference is that in "zhèr shì shū" it means that there is nothing else but
books, and "zhèr yǒu shū" means that there are books but also something
else. This is one thing. And the other feature is that if you say "zhèr yǒu
shū" it means that there are some books, not all the books are there. If
you add "suǒ" in that case it means the totality. There is a change of contents and an opposition between "yǒu" and "suǒ yǒu" which is absolutely
unique.

Søren Egerod

THE TYPOLOGY OF ARCHAIC CHINESE

It has become clear through recent advances made in the field of Archaic
Chinese reconstruction that consonant clusters play an important role not
only in the phonetic typology (phonemics) of the language but also in the
morphological typology (morphophonemics). The clusters containing a
retroflex feature ("r"), a lateral feature ("l"), a palatal feature ("j"), or
a nasal feature ("n") in their second element alternate with simple consonants (祫 gɛp <grəp 'sacrifice to spirits collectively': 合 gəp
'unite', cf Tai grop 'complete': gop 'associate with'), (勍 gljǎn
'strong': 競 gjǎŋ 'vigorously'), (入 ńjəp 'enter': 內 nəp 'bring
in', cf Tai hnep 'insert'), (須 sju 'wait': 需 snju 'tarry'). A labial
nasal probably functions both as a prefix and as an infix (繆 mljŏg
'bind around': 摎 ljŏg ~ kljŏg 'tie around, strangle') (摩 hmwia
'a signal': 撝 hwia 'to signal'). A labial stop functions as a prefix
(廩 ljəm 'granary': 稟 pljəm 'rations'), just as there are traces
of dental and velar stop prefixes. If the voiced stops "b", "d", and "g"
are considered as containing a voiced aspirated feature ("ɦ") this feature
also can be said to function as an infix (合 gəp = khəp 'unite, shut':
闔 kəp 'gate'). There was a system of suffixes reflected in the development of the tonal system.

157

These phonemic and morphophonemic typological characteristics clearly remind us of similar phenomena in several other languages, especially Malayo-Polynesian and Mon-Khmer. It will therefore be of interest to test other typological features of Archaic Chinese for agreement with these languages. The following is a sketch of the syntactic typology of the Lu dialect of Archaic Chinese, according to the same pattern and terminology as that used in my article on Atayal Grammar in Lg 42 (66) 346-369. The most important features called to our attention here are the pronominalizing nature of the language and its use of noun incorporation, which in spite of the difference in word order is quite parallel in Malayo-Polynesian and in Archaic Chinese. These facts are offered as a supplement to the arguments, based on comparison of vocabulary, which were set forth by Kurt Wulff in his "Über das verhältnis des malayo-polynesischen zum indochinesischen" (1942).

The Archaic Chinese Sentence consists of an Exposure[1] and a Predicate[2]. The Exposure may contain an Initial Particle (雖 etc, closed class), the Predicate a Final Particle (乎 etc, closed class). There may be a Middle Particle (則 etc, closed class) between the Exposure and the Predicate. The Exposure is a Primary Pronoun I, II, or III, a Quasi-Pronoun, or a Verbal Construct. The Predicate is a Primary Pronoun I or II, a Quasi-Pronoun, or a Verbal Construct. The Primary Pronouns are I 我 , II 汝 , III zero. The Quasi-Pronouns are Modifiable Nouns (人 君 , 馬 etc, open class), preceded or not by their Noun Modifiers, and Nonmodifiable Nouns (是 , 此 , 彼 etc and Personal Names, closed class). The Verbal Construct consists of the Verb (好 , 治 , 樂 etc, open class), preceded or not by an Agent and/or a Verb Modifier, followed or not by an Object and/or a Verb Complement. Noun Modifiers are Secondary Pronouns I, II, or III, Modifiable Nouns followed or not by 之 , Nonmodifiable Nouns, Nonmodifiable Noun Modifiers (夫 , 斯 etc, closed class), or Verbs followed or not by an Object[3]. The Secondary Pronouns are I 吾 , II 爾 , III 其 . Verb Modifiers are Verbal Constructs followed or not by 而 , Modifiable Nouns followed or not by 而 , Primary Pronouns or Quasi-Pronouns preceded by Nonmodifiable Verbs (以 , 與 , 自 etc, closed class), or Nonmodifiable Verb Modifiers (不 etc, closed class). The Agent is an Agential Pronoun or a Quasi-Pronoun. The Agential Pronouns are I 吾 , II 爾 , III zero. The Object is an Objective Pronoun or a Quasi-Pronoun or both, or a Verb followed or not by an Object[3]. The Objective Pronouns are I 我 , II 汝 , III 之 . The Verb Complement is an Objective Pronoun preceded by 於 , or a Quasi-Pronoun preceded by 於 . 於 plus the Objective Pronoun 之 combine as 焉 . The Objective Pronoun 之 plus 於 combine as 諸 .

Verbs are Intransitive and potentially Causative (– Putative) (好 ~ 好˙) or Transitive (Active and Passive) and potentially Resultative Passive (.治 ~ 治˙), or Transitive (Active and Causative Passive) and potentially Resultative Passive (.覿 ~ 覿˙), or Causative (Active and

159

Causative Passive) (悅)[4]. The Agent of a Transitive Verb may appear as the Complement of a Passive Verb. The Object of a Transitive Verb may appear as the Agent of a Passive Verb. The Object of a Transitive Verb may appear as the Complement of a Causative Passive Verb.

Either the Exposure or the Predicate may be followed by 也 . A Modifiable Noun may be followed by 者 and a Verbal Construct by 矣 . 矣 combines the semantic content of 已 'verbal completion' and of 也 'end of Exposure or Predicate', and cannot itself be followed by 也 . The potential Agent of a Verb may enter another sentence as a Quasi-Pronoun, in which case the Verb is followed by 者 . The potential Object or Complement of a Verb may enter another sentence as a Quasi-Pronoun, in which case the Verb is preceded by 所 . The potential Verb in a Verbal Construct may enter another sentence as a Verb, in which case a Quasi-Pronoun is followed by 矣 .

A Verbal Construct may function as a Quasi-Pronoun, in which case the Agent becomes a Noun Modifier (the Pronominal Agent changes from Agential to Secondary form and the Quasi-Pronominal Agent may add 之). Under similar circumstances the Object may also become a Noun Modifier, preceding the Verb. A Verbal Construct may function as a Verb Modifier, in which case the Quasi-Pronominal Agent becomes a Verb Modifier (followed or not by 而). Under similar circumstances the Object may also become a Verb Modifier preceding the Verb.[5]

1. Sentences without an Exposure are rather rare (e.g. LY 1.4 吾日 三省吾身) and should not be confused with Sentences whose Exposure is a Primary Pronoun III manifested as Zero (e.g. LY 8.13 耻也).

2. Both Exposure and Predicate can be constituted as Verbal by means of specific syntactic constructions. In LY 1.1 人不知而不慍 the Potential Exposure 人不知 is Verbal because followed by 而 . This construction is reminiscent of the transformation which allows an Object to be incorporated in the Verb by means of 而 (see footnote 5 below). In LY 1.2 其為人也 the Potential Predicate 人 is constituted as Verbal by means of 為 which takes an Agential Pronoun III. 人 is not an Object because the Objective Pronoun 之 could not be found after 為 in this sense. In LY 1.1 人不知而不慍不亦君子乎 the Predicate 君子 is manifested as Verbal by means of 不 (what is negated is not 君子 , but the relation between Exposure and Predicate).

3. A Verb followed or not by an Object but not modifiable by an Agent is a Minor Verbal Construct. A Minor Verbal Construct occurs as Noun Modifier (e.g. Menc 1 A 7 是折枝之類也) and as Object (e.g. 1.1 不好犯上).

4.

Intransitive	Causative (-Putative)	Transitive	Passive	Causative Passive	Resultative Passive
好	好˙	王治民	民治於王		民治˙
遠	遠˙				
事成	成事				
	悅人			悅於人	
		觀人		觀於人	觀˙

5. The Transformations involved can be summarized as follows:

$N^A V$	> N : N	V	王好樂	王之好樂
[AP V	> N : SP	V	好樂	其好樂]
$V N^O$	> N : N	V	用礼	礼之用
$N^A V$	> V : N	V	言有信	言而有信
$V N^O$	> V : N	V	分資財	資財而分
[$V N^{VC}$	> V : N	V	廢於中道	中道而廢]

BIBLIOGRAPHY

Bodman	Shih Ming, HYIS 11 (54)
	rev R A Miller TP 44 (56) 266–287
Boodberg	Proleptic, HJAS 2 (37) 329–372
Chao, Y.R.	rev Grammata Serica Lg 17 (41) 60–67
Chmielewski	Syntax, RO 28 (64) 107–125
Chou Fa-kao	On the Phonology of Archaic Chinese, JICSCUHK 2 (69) 109–178
Dobson	EAC 1962
	LAC 1959
	rev Egerod AO (60) 173–179
Egerod	Atayal, Lg 42 (66) 346–369
	Les particularités de la grammaire chinoise (in print)
Forrest	The Chinese Language 1965[2]
	Reconsideration, TP 51 (64) 229–246
	Researches, ZDMG 111 (61) 118–138
Gabelentz	Chinesische Grammatik 1960[2]
Grube	Die sprachgeschichtliche Stellung 1881
Haudricourt	Comment reconstruire, Word 10 (54) 351–364
Jacob	Strcuture of the Word in Old Khmer, BSOAS 23 (60) 351–368
Karlgren	Cognate Words, BMFEA 28 (56) 1–19
	Word Families, BMFEA 5 (33) 9–121
Li	Some Old Chinese Loan Words, HJAS 8 (49) 333–342
Maspero	Langues thai, chinois etc., Langue du Monde 1952
	Préfixes et dérivation, MSLP 23 (35) 313–327
Pinnow	Historische Lautlehre der Kharia-Sprache 1959
Pulleyblank	Consonantal System, AM NS 9 (62) 58–144 and 9 (62) 206–265
Sedláček	Initial clusters, Orbis 13 (64) 556–567
	Über das *-r-, CAJ 9 (64) 203–223
Tung T'ung-ho	Shang-ku yin-yün, CYYY 18 (48) 1–249
Wolfenden	Outlines 1929
Wulff	Chinesisch und Thai 1934
	rev Maspero BSLP 36 (35) 183–187
	Musik und Freude 1935
	Über das verhältnis 1942

Agent =   Agential Pronoun
                                 Quasi-Pronoun

                                 The Object of a Transitive Verb may appear
                                 as the Agent of a Passive Verb.

Agential Pronoun =   I 吾 , II 爾 , III zero

Exposure =   Primary Pronoun I, II III
                                 Quasi-Pronoun
                                 Verbal Construct

                                 May contain an Initial Particle.

                                 May be followed by 也 (if the Predicate is not

                                 followed by 也).

Final Particle =   乎 etc, closed class

Initial Particle =   雖 etc, closed class

Middle Particle =   則 etc, closed class

                                 There may be a Middle Particle between the
                                 Exposure and the Predicate.

Minor Verbal
Construct =   Verbs followed or not by an Object but not
                                 modifiable by an Agent

Modifiable Nouns =   人 , 君 , 馬 etc, open class

                                 May be followed by 者 .

Nonmodifiable Nouns =   是 , 此 , 彼 etc, and Personal Names,
                                 closed class

Nonmodifiable Noun
Modifiers =   夫 , 斯 etc, closed class

Nonmodifiable Verbs = 以 , 與 , 曰 etc, closed class

Nonmodifiable Verb
Modifiers = 不 etc, closed class

Noun Modifiers =
Secondary Pronouns I, II, III,
Modifiable Nouns followed or not by 之
Nonmodifiable Nouns
Nonmodifiable Noun Modifiers
Minor Verbal Constructs

When a Verbal Construct functions as a Quasi-
Pronoun the Quasi-Pronominal Object may become
a Noun Modifier followed by 之 , preceding
the Verb.

Object =
Objective Pronoun and/or Quasi-Pronoun
Verb followed or not by an Object

Objective Pronoun = I 我 , II 汝 , III 之

Predicate =
Primary Pronoun I, II
Quasi-Pronoun
Verbal Construct

May contain a Final Particle

May be followed by 也 (if the Exposure is not
followed by 也).

Primary Pronouns = I 我 , II 汝 , III zero

Quasi-Pronouns =
Modifiable Nouns preceded or not by their Noun
Modifiers
Nonmodifiable Nouns

The potential Agent of a Verb may enter another
sentence as a Quasi-Pronoun, in which case the
Verb is followed by 者 .

The potential Object or Complement of a Verb
may enter another sentence as a Quasi-Pronoun,
in which case the Verb is preceded by 所 .

165

A Verbal Construct may function as a Quasi-
Pronoun in which case the Agent becomes a Noun
Modifier (the Pronominal Agent changes from
Agential to Secondary form and the Quasi-Pronom-
inal Agent most often adds 之). Under similar
circumstánces the Object may also become a
Noun Modifier, preceding the Verb.

Secondary Pronoun =   I 吾 , II 汝 , III zero.

Verbs =   好 , 治 , 樂 etc, open class.

Intransitive and potentially Causative (-Putative)
(好̇ , 好̇)

Transitive (Active and Passive) and potentially
Resultative Passive (.̇治 , 治̇).

Transitive (Active and Causative Passive) and
potentially Resultative Passive (.̇覯 , 覯̇).

Causative (Active and Causative Passive) (悦).

The potential Verb in a Verbal Construct may enter
another sentence as a Verb, in which case a
Quasi-Pronoun is followed by 矣 .

Verb Complement =   Objective Pronoun preceded by 於 .
Quasi-Pronoun preceded by 於 .
(於 + 之 = 焉 , 之 + 於 = 諸).

The Agent of a Transitive Verb may appear as
the Complement of a Passive Verb.

The Object of a Transitive Verb may appear as
the Complement of a Passive Verb.

Verbal Construct =   Verb preceded or not by an Agent and/or a Verb
Modifier followed or not by an Object and/or a
Verb Complement.

May be followed by 矣

166

Verb Modifier =

Verbal Constructs followed or not by कर .
Modifiable Nouns followed or not by कर .
Primary Pronouns or Quasi-Pronouns preceded
by Nonmodifiable Verbs
Nonmodifiable Verb Modifiers

A Verbal Construct may function as a Verb Modifier in which case the Quasi-Pronominal Agent
becomes a Verb Modifier (followed or not by कर).
Under similar circumstances the Object may also
become a Verb Modifier preceding the Verb.

DISCUSSION ON EGEROD'S PAPER: THE TYPOLOGY OF ARCHAIC CHINESE

Malmqvist: I think it would be very hard to find out whether in fact what you have is a causative passive or simply plain causative. The only example

you have is 觀 . The only example I could think of is the story in the Chunqiu when the Duke of Lǔ is travelling to Qí to have a look at the shè-sacrifices, and the Gongyang zhuan says: "why did you go there. Why did you go to have a look at the shè". And then continues that he did not go there to have a look at the shè and says "yǐ guān fù rén yě". Now, he went there either to cause his women to be looked at, to show up his women, or to cause the woman to have a look at the "shè".

Egerod: I do not mind if this can also be the other interpretation. We could perhaps make another column. I admit that since there are often no formal criteria we are sometimes not quite sure where to put it.

Malmqvist: What is the Lu dialect?

Egerod: That I don't quite know. I am referring to Karlgren's usage, of course. I have not used any examples outside the Lunyu and Mencius. I haven't used the Zuozhuan.

Graham: I would like to ask about the Primary and Secondary Pronouns. In the 2nd person I think that Karlgren made the distinction the other way round. But Dobson did take your position on the evidence of the Zuozhuan.

Egerod: Yes, I am aware of that problem. It is unfortunately to a certain degree a statistical problem and not quite as clear as the 1st person. For phonetic reasons I like this one better than the original one, but I should not use that as an argument for putting it here.

Graham: You have Nounmodifiers as Secondary Pronouns I, II or III. Presumably 我 is sometimes a Nounmodifier, e.g. 我 心 "my heart", but 我 is a Primary Pronoun in your system.

Egerod: Aha, that's right. That would take a note. Under what circum-stances is this 我 Secondary is a question to answer.

Malmqvist: You say that 乎 can be a Final Particle in the Predicate. Does that exclude 乎 from being a Final Particle of the Exposure?

Egerod: No, certainly not. The difficult class of these three seems to me to be the Middle Particle, which should have the property of constituting

a relationship between two things, and I think that 則 is a quite good example of that. And they don't behave alike in word order. All particles almost are one-word word classes that have to be treated specially.

Graham: I would like to ask about "the potential verb in a Verbal Construct may enter another sentence as a Verb, in which case a Quasi-Pronoun is

followed by 矣 ". I suppose this would be the example "wǔ shì yǐ", "five generations" wouldn't it?

Egerod: The one that contains a number, yes. Somehow it is probably tied up with the fact that there is a number, which is a constraint on that con-struction which is interesting, and it seems to be true of modern Chinese too, where you have "sān suì" and "sān suì le" which is exactly the same phenomenon. And this has to be expressed when you describe your numerals that they can do this, but it is still the noun that receives the "yǐ" and not the numeral.

Graham: I was wondering because these numeral expressions like "wǔ shì" are difficult to deal with nominally or verbally, and they appear in many contexts without any "yǐ", e.g. something like "mǎ sì zú", "a horse has four feet". I don't think it would have a "yǐ". In this case it seems to me as if it has something to do with the five generations being counted off or something.

Egerod: Exactly. That is that verbal element which is not expressed, but which you have to assume is there in order to make sense out of it. You can have, say, the 3rd person pronoun which is never there on the surface, the Primary is always zero in the 3rd person, but there is a content which we have to deal with in order to understand the sentence. The same is true in such a construction where there is a potential verbal construct which we cannot get up to the surface, because it is never expressed, but we must assume it is there, firstly because "yǐ" is there, secondly in order to make sense out of the sentence. It has a semantic content, something like "elapse", but it is not identical with any known Chinese word.

Graham: How would you take it in a case like "mǎ sì zú". I don't think one would say "mǎ yǒu sì zú".

Egerod: No, I would say that the "mǎ" must be an Exposure, "as for the horse", and then we have a statement that its characteristic is having four legs. We cannot say that there is anything missing which we can assign a a word to, but we must describe it as a property of this noun that we can enter it into this Exposure-Predicate construction without "yǒu".

Rygaloff: Doesn't the verb come out in the negative form, "tā méi yǒu èr shí suì le" or "tā bú shì èr shí suì le"?

Egerod: I guess you would get a "méi yǒu" also here. If we wanted to say that the legs were long we would put the adjective after the noun, wouldn't we? But it is a property of the numerals that they are incorporated into the noun. Instead of being predicates they are noun modifiers and this has as a result that the sentence looks like that. If we said that we started from a sentence that said that the legs are four, then we just have to realize that it is in the deep structure only and on the surface this will not be said. I think it is true that you have to make special statements with numerals which give us other kinds of departure.

Malmqvist: I am wondering about the Nonmodifiable Verb Modifiers. I am trying to find a modifiable "bù".

Graham: What about "bì bù", "certainly not"?

Egerod: Do you think that "bì" modifies "bù" or "bù" plus the verb?

Graham: Yes I agree that that is a question.

Egerod: Like "not big at all", Does "at all" modify "not" or "not big".

Graham: I wonder about what you say about "yǐ", that it combines the semantic content of "yǐ" and "yě". What semantic content of "yě" is included in "yǐ"?

Egerod: I meant in terms of what I have said in my other paper "Les particularités de la grammaire chinoise" that the function of "yě" is to give what I have called "vertical signals", that we have to restrict ourselves to those signals. This is also true of "yǐ", but at the same time it is true of "yǐ" that it adds something else which for one thing has a semantic content like completion, and secondly can combine only with a verb. My theory is that

the "yĕ" has no other contents than that of indicating either an Exposure
or a Predicate or a combination of the two, but the "yǐ" probably has some
contents besides that, something like completion or whatever it is.

Graham: In many sentences one would feel the content altered by "yĕ". I
am not suggesting that it does that every time. In "bù néng yĕ" it is not
merely "I am not able" but "It's that I am not able". Something changes with
the use of "yĕ".

Egerod: I think I made more or less the same point in connection with "yĕ
zhĕ" where "rén zhĕ" might be the one who is benevolent, but "rén yĕ zhĕ"
can only be "being benevolent". We can say that both are verbal but one
refers to the one "who is", and the other just to "being". Then it would be
more or less the same here where you get "being able to" rather than some
specific person who "is able to". In a way you can say that "yĕ" makes impossible a transformation. If we have the "zhĕ","zhĕ" can either express a
transformation, that is it says, take the subject of this verb and make it into
a noun in another sentence "cóng zhĕ","he who follows". It can also just
insist on the signals that are present in a noun "zòng zhĕ", "a follower"
written by means of the same character. There it is interesting to see then
that if you put the "yĕ" before "zhĕ", and say "rén yĕ zhĕ", then it does
exactly this that it indicates there must be no transformation here, it must
not be "he who is good", it must be "being good" and then something about
that. It is directly a subject, it is not transformed into a subject. So I would
say that one signal given by "yĕ" is "avoid transformation", "yĕ" can never
indicate a transformation but "zhĕ" can.

Rygaloff: I am struck with the two first formulas which are exactly what I
was leading to this morning. This is what I started with and then I made
some preliminary transformations.

Egerod: What my first one says in terms of Chinese is that "the king loves
music", and then if you pu "zhī" between "the king" and "love" then you get
"the fact that the king loves music". That is not related to either "the king"
or "the music" being present in another sentence. You don't combine this
with another sentence where there is another king or another music.

Rygaloff: Yes, but you can use it in a sentence where it fits.

Egerod: The special thing about your example is that there is a word
common to two sentences. This is not the construction "the music that
the king loves is good", it is "the fact that the king loves music".

Rygaloff: Then the second example would be more fit. It is the same type of operation. You are correlating a nominal phrase with an underlying sentence, this is exactly what I was trying to do. The comments I was making about the contents was about a difference of level, because as long as you consider the underlying sentence there is some content in this respect in the sentence. Of course when you consider the nominal phrase which is derived it has no content in this respect itself. It has to be in a sentence to get one, to have definite or indefinite reference. But independently of what content it may have in a sentence it has some implications in relation to the underlying sentence and this is what I was saying. "Students who like wine" imply that some students don't and this has to be accounted for in the underlying sentence. This is of course not the point but I am struck by the mechanism which I think is the same.

Egerod: When you say that you have a king who loves music, then he is the agent and the music the object. Then you can say "love music zhī king" but in the Mencius and the Lunyu you don't find "the king loves zhī music". you don't find "S V zhī N", which is the construction you are concerned with in modern Chinese. You don't find "wáng hào zhī ... (N)" and that is why I call this a minor verbal construct where you can't have an agent. In later Chinese you get this construction, but you are faced with the problem that you are no longer working with one underlying sentence but two.

Graham: I would like to ask about the modal "qí". I wonder how you feel historically about there being another pronoun "júe" in the preclassical and the fact that modal "qí" seems to be more common than the pronoun "qí" in the preclassical. There is also the question of "qí" after a personal pronoun. I am thinking of David S. Nivison's paper: "So-called modal ch'i in classical Chinese".

Egerod: I do think that it is a similar point that I have tried to make. I find in his paper that the so-called modal "qí" of course, since it is supposed to be modal, turns out in sentences which are exclamations, or emphatic questions and so on. Then it is the question, is it the "qí" that makes these sentences modal or is it rather that we tend to get a subordinating pronoun in such sentences just as such things in other languages tend to look like subordinate sentences. In Latin you say the whole thing in accusative as if it were governed by a "videte" or something which actually isn't there. So my question is, isn't it more likely that the type of sentence to which all of these belong have a 3rd person pronoun expressed. And then later when the 3rd person pronoun isn't really used like that at all then people start misunderstanding it and reading it as if it were the pronoun that were modal, when actually it is the sentence that calls for a pronoun. I sort of feel that it is true that at a certain point modal "qí" started to come up but

172

I think from a misunderstanding of those classical sentences where it was present for other reasons. That's why I agree with Nivison. It seems to me that there is such a similarity in all the sentences and then it is easier to think that it is the pronoun that is called for by the similarities of the sentences than the other way round. I don't agree with his phonological speculations but I like his semantic speculations the more since I have really once suggested the same thing myself in a paper on Chuang-tzu (AO 25.1960. 112-120). At that time I was so convinced that I was right that I wrote about the myth of modal "qí". I am very much attracted by Chou Fa-kao who thinks that it is the present-day Cantonese 3rd person pronoun which is hidden in those forms.

Graham: Yes, it fits well. I wonder whether there may always have been a 3rd person pronoun in the spoken language.

Egerod: In so many Malay languages you have something parallel. That is one of the reasons why I tried to do this analysis as close to a Malay language I could. That was why I was happy that Malmqvist came up with these l's and m's, and n's yesterday and called them infixes. If people like Wulff are at all right that they are related we would like to find much more than what we have, and if I am right that there is a similarity in the pronominal structure it would not be a bad indication.

Rygaloff: In many languages the 3rd person pronoun is something like "this man" as in Japanese "ano hito" and in Mongol too.

Graham: I can't get away from the suspicion that there must have been some way of saying it a bit more regularly.

Egerod: In Malay where the passive is construed with possessive pronouns the third person works differently from the two others. What I am driving at is of course that I would like to find indications that the passive is original in classical Chinese, and that is why we have the possessive pronoun even in complete statements, and the 3rd person is different exactly as Malay. We meet Chinese when it is in the transitional period between two types of constructions which develop quite differently but I am intrigued by these several indications, beyond Wulff's and Benedict's and others' lists of words that may be related, that you also find in the grammar several indications of the same behavior with verbs in relation to pronouns with even the same classes that come out when you squeeze the pattern. I am also intrigued by the infixes. There are quite a few treatments of infixes in classical Chinese, but I don't know of anybody who has tried to give a semantic content to the infixes, and I have just in a very small way tried to find as many indications as I can. When we have two forms and Karlgren posits, say, an "n" in one of them, according to Wulff the "n" is in the other one. Whichever one has the infix sometimes it seems to me that you can glimpse the difference in meaning, but one have to go through an awful lot of texts before one dare say anything. If there is anything in this it goes well with the indications of the pronouns here.

Malmqvist: In the Zuozhuan you can find instances of N zhi V constructions in apparantly independant sentences containing a final particle "yǐ" or "hǔ". That construction seems to have a moment of modality in it. It seems to have the same function as the so-called modal "qí". On the other hand Chou Fa-kao has described a lot of instances of "qí" substituting for "zhī", and there you may have a connection.

Egerod: I tend to go in the direction of Nivison but it has to be worked out further.

Egerod: So what this all seems to show is that while on one hand we have seen Chinese typologically go from almost one extreme to another we have in some of the very basic syntactic relationships found perhaps more unity than we would have suspected and I was at least surprised; I don't know if I should have been.

THE SCANDINAVIAN INSTITUTE OF ASIAN STUDIES

Founded 1967

2, Kejsergade   1155 Copenhagen K   Denmark

Board

Professor Pentti Aalto, Finland (Vice-Chairman)
Professor Jussi Aro, Finland
Dr. Philos. Otto Chr. Dahl, Norway
Professor Kristof Glamann, Denmark
Professor Henry Henne, Norway
Professor K. G. Izikowitz, Sweden
Professor Göran Malmqvist, Sweden (Chairman)
Professor Anders Ølgaard, Denmark

Director

Professor Søren Egerod, Denmark

Fellows

Karl Reinhold Haellquist, Fil. lic.
Benedicte Hjejle, M. A., D, Phil. (Oxon)
Trygve Lötveit, M. A., Ph. D.
Poul Mohr, M. A.
Asko Parpola, M. A., Ph. D.
Per Sørensen, M. A.

Librarian

Eric Douglas Grinstead, B. A.

Assistant Librarians

Hanne Balslev
Ib Norel

Secretaries

Setsuko Bergholdt-Hansen
Susanna Harald Hansen
Ulla Kasten

Contents

Scandinavian Institute of Asian Studies Monograph Series